E-Z PLAY GUITAR

EASY TO READ NOTES WITH TABLATURE

Gospel Songs To Live By

WITHDRAWN

ISBN 0-634-01575-3

HAL•LEONARD®
CORPORATION

7777 W. BLUEMOUND RD. P.O. BOX 13819 MILWAUKEE, WI 53213

E-Z Play® Today Music Notation © 1975 by HAL LEONARD CORPORATION

E-Z PLAY and EASY ELECTRONIC KEYBOARD MUSIC are registered trademarks of HAL LEONARD CORPORATION.

Visit Hal Leonard Online at
www.halleonard.com

Gospel Songs To Live By

CONTENTS

STRUM AND PICK PATTERNS

This chart contains the suggested strum and pick patterns that are referred to by number at the beginning of each song in this book. The symbols ⊓ and ∨ in the strum patterns refer to down and up strokes, respectively. The letters in the pick patterns indicate which right-hand fingers plays which strings.

p = thumb
i = index finger
m = middle finger
a = ring finger

For example; Pick Pattern 2
is played: thumb - index - middle - ring

Strum Patterns   Pick Patterns

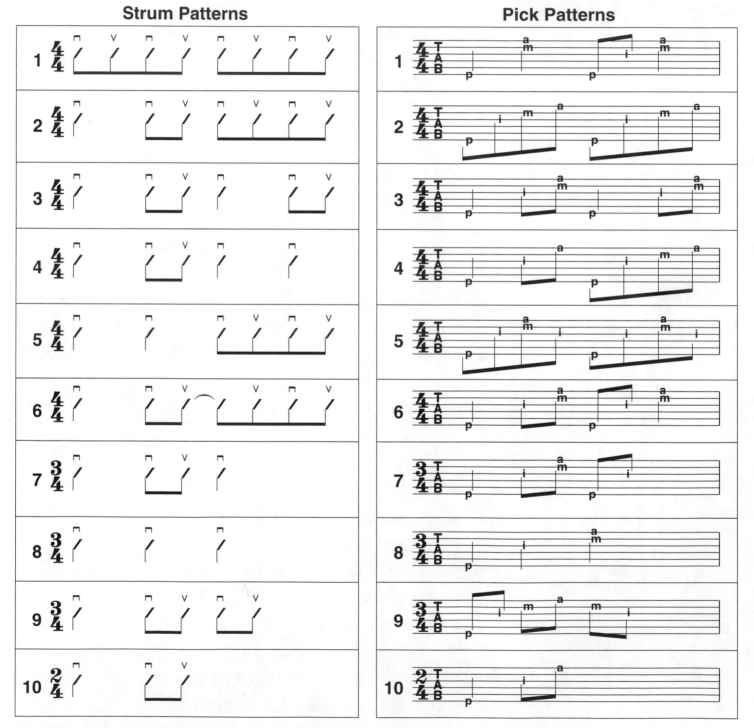

You can use the 3/4 Strum or Pick Patterns in songs written in compound meter (6/8, 9/8, 12/8, etc.).
For example, you can accompany a song in 6/8 by playing the 3/4 pattern twice in each measure.
The 4/4 Strum and Pick Patterns can be used for songs written in cut time (¢) by doubling the note time values in the patterns. Each pattern would therefore last two measures in cut time.

Blessed Assurance

Lyrics by Fanny Crosby and Van Alstyne
Music by Phoebe P. Knapp

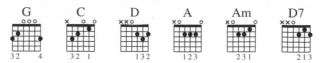

Strum Pattern: 8
Pick Pattern: 8

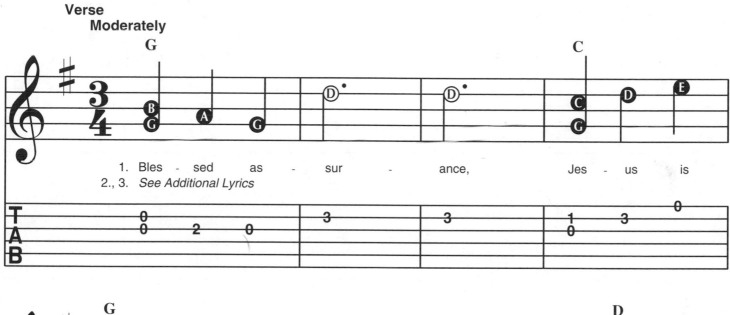

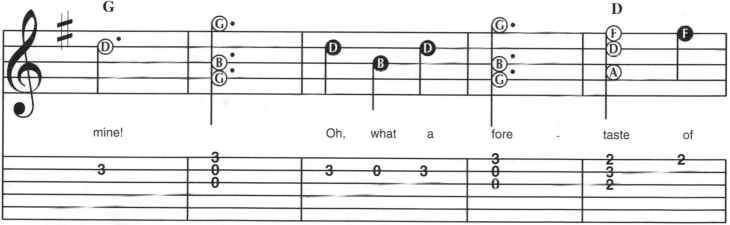

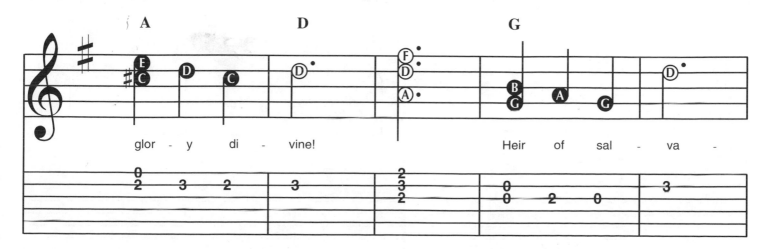

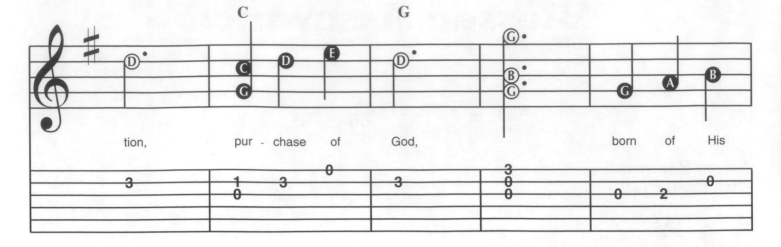

tion,   pur - chase of God,   born of His

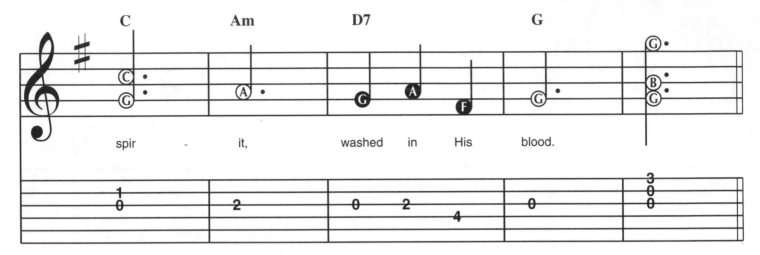

spir - it,   washed   in   His   blood.

Chorus

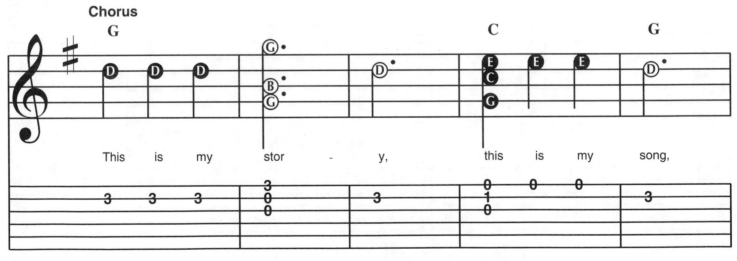

This   is   my   stor - y,   this   is   my   song,

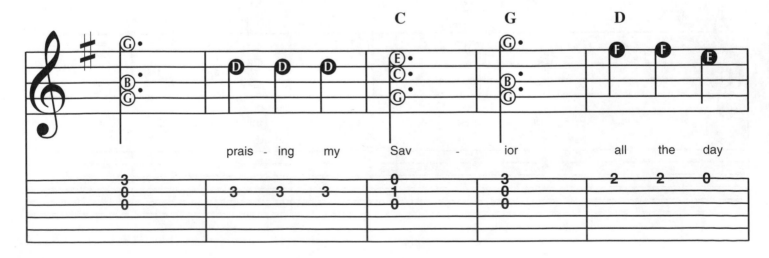

prais - ing   my   Sav - ior   all   the   day

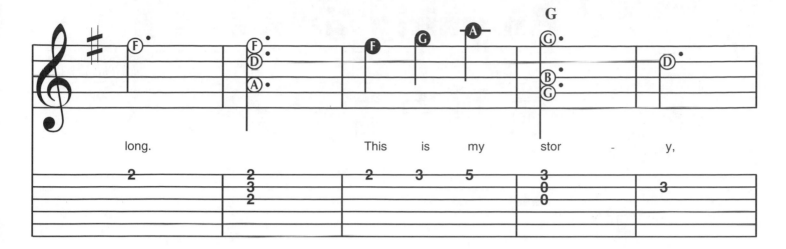

long.   This   is   my   stor - y,

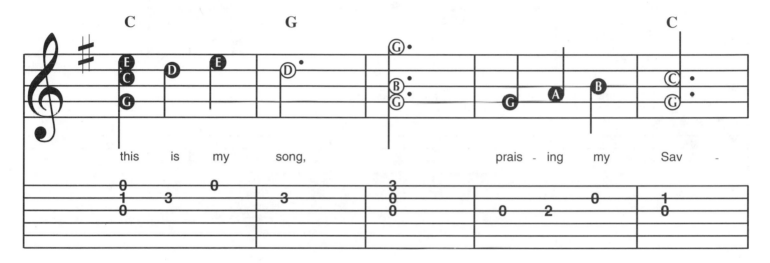

this   is   my   song,   prais - ing   my   Sav -

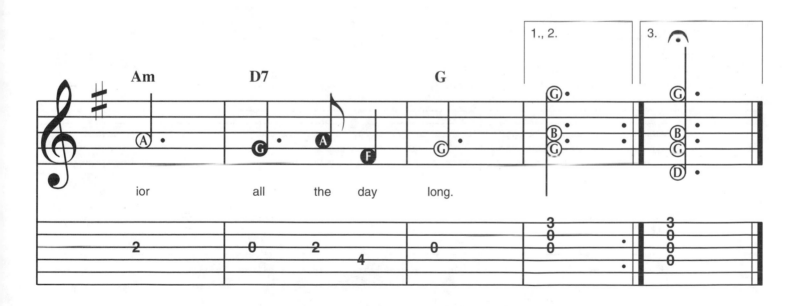

ior   all   the   day   long.

Additional Lyrics

2. Perfect submission, perfect delight,
   Visions of rapture now burst on my sight.
   Angels descending, bring from above
   Echoes of mercy, whispers of love.

3. Perfect submission, all is at rest.
   I in my Savior am happy and blest.
   Watching and waiting, looking above,
   Filled with His goodness, lost in His love.

Amazing Grace

Words by John Newton
Traditional American Melody

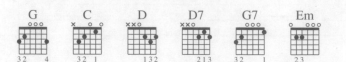

Strum Pattern: 7
Pick Pattern: 7

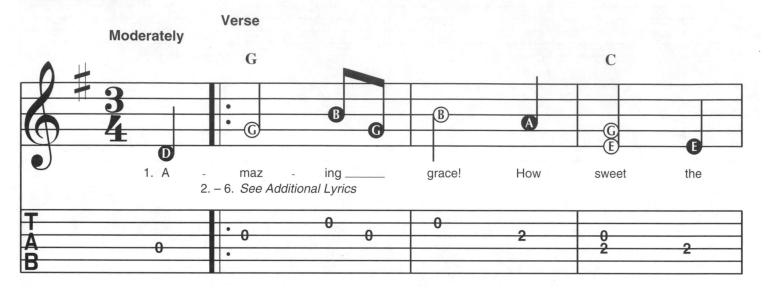

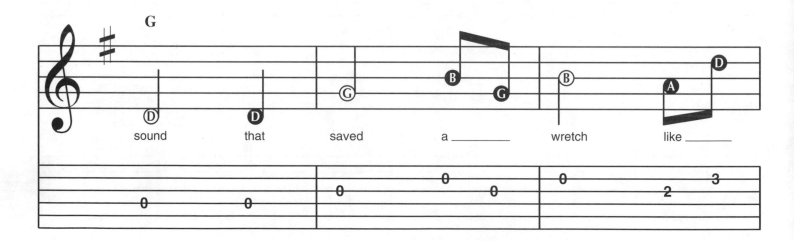

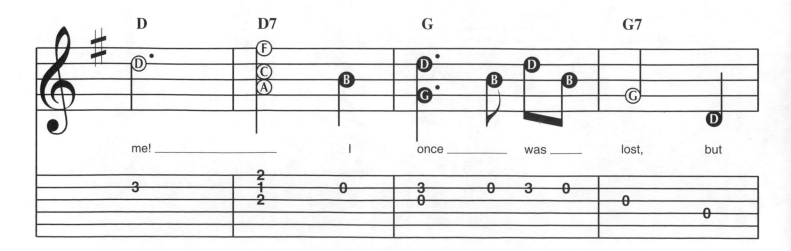

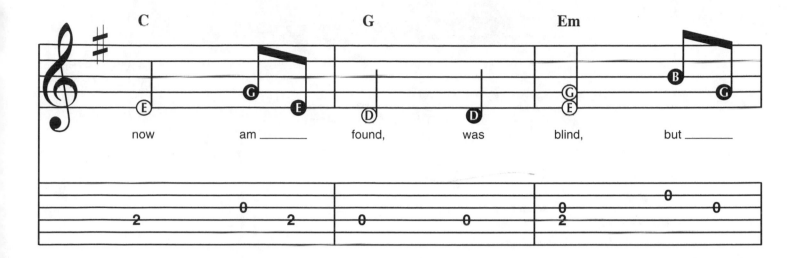

now   am _____ found,   was   blind,   but _____

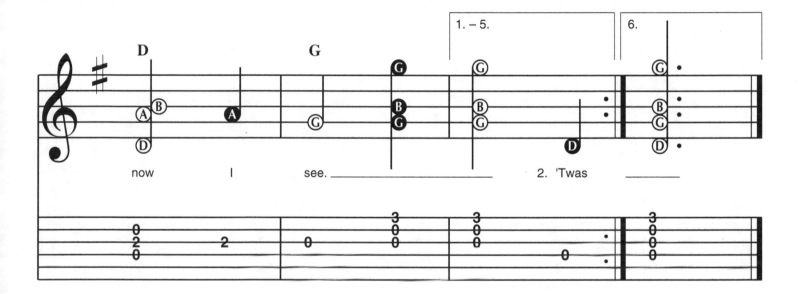

now   I   see. _____   2. 'Twas _____

Additional Lyrics

2. 'Twas grace that taught my heart to fear,
   And grace my fears relieved.
   How precious did that grace appear
   The hour I first believed.

3. Through many dangers, toils and snares,
   I have already come.
   'Tis grace has brought me safe thus far,
   And grace will lead me home.

4. The Lord has promised good to me,
   His word my hope secures.
   He will my shield and portion be
   As long as life endures.

5. And when this flesh and heart shall fail,
   And mortal life shall cease.
   I shall possess within the veil
   A life of joy and peace.

6. When we've been there ten thousand years,
   Bright shining as the sun.
   We've no less days to sing God's praise
   Than when we first begun.

At Calvary

Words by William R. Newell
Music by Daniel B. Towner

Strum Pattern: 4
Pick Pattern: 4

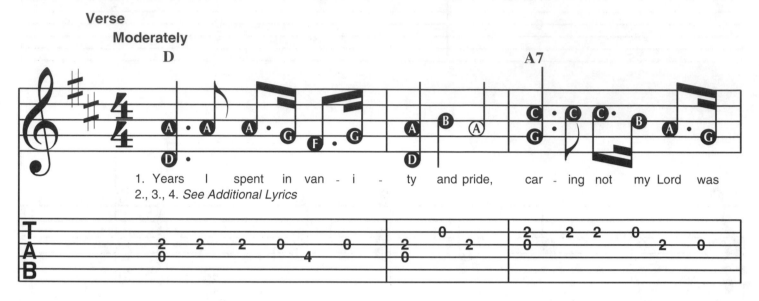

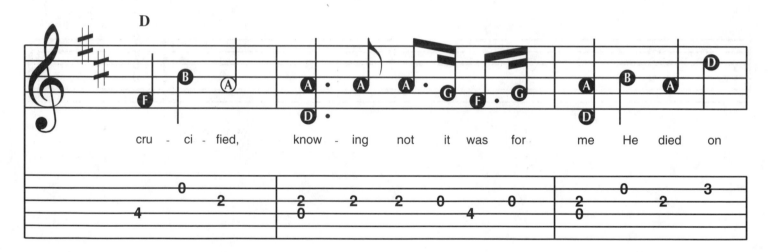

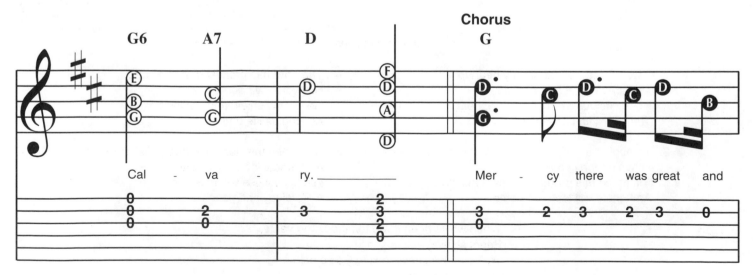

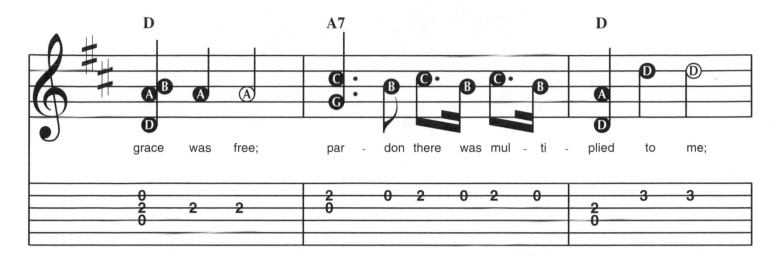

grace was free; par - don there was mul - ti - plied to me;

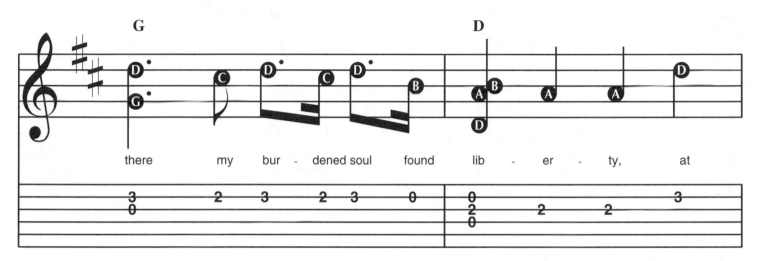

there my bur - dened soul found lib - er - ty, at

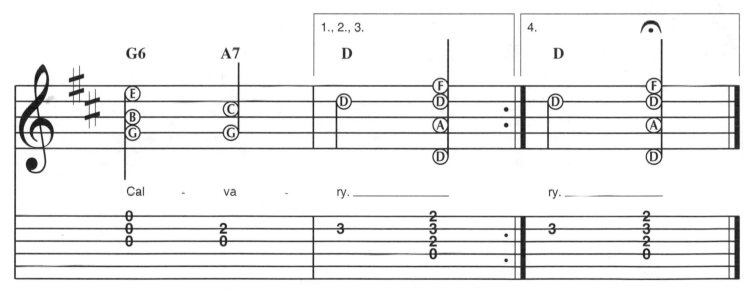

Cal - va - ry. _____   ry. _____

Additional Lyrics

2. By God's Word at last my sin I learned;
   Then I trembled at the law I'd spurned,
   Till my guilty soul imploring turned to Calvary.

3. Now I've giv'n to Jesus ev'rything;
   Now I gladly own Him as my King;
   Now my raptured soul can only sing of Calvary.

4. O the love that drew salvation's plan!
   O the grace that brought it down to man!
   O the mighty gulf that God did span at Calvary!

At the Cross

Text by Isaac Watts
Music by Ralph E. Hudson

Strum Pattern: 2
Pick Pattern: 4

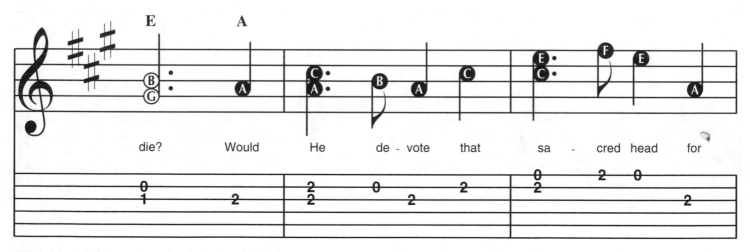

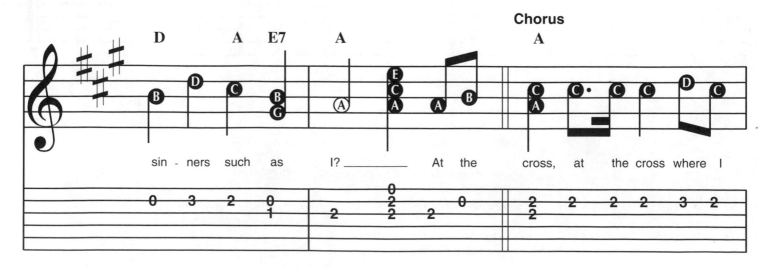

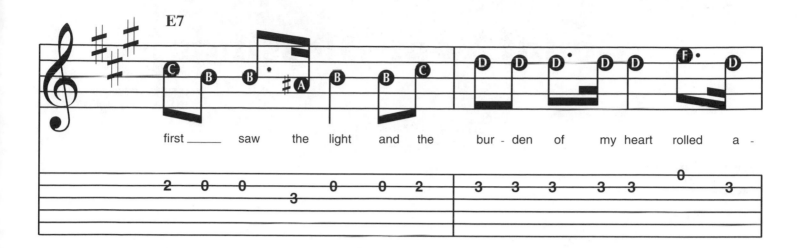

first _____ saw the light and the bur - den of my heart rolled a -

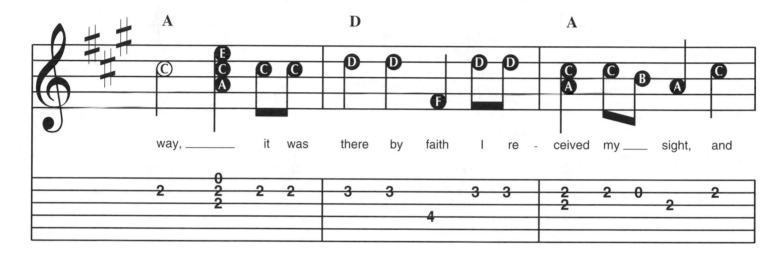

way, _____ it was there by faith I re - ceived my _____ sight, and

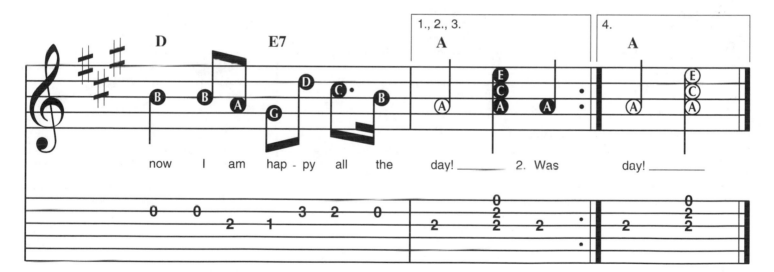

now I am hap - py all the day! _____ 2. Was day! _____

Additional Lyrics

2. Was it for crimes that I have done He groaned upon the tree?
   Amazing pity! Grace unknown! And love beyond degree!

3. Well might the sun in darkness hole and shut His glories in,
   When Christ, the mighty Maker, died for man the creature's sin.

4. But drops of grief can ne'er repay the debt of love I owe:
   Here, Lord, I give myself away; 'tis all that I can do!

Count Your Blessings

Words by Johnson Oatman, Jr.
Music by Edwin O. Excell

Strum Pattern: 10
Pick Pattern: 10

Verse
Moderately Slow

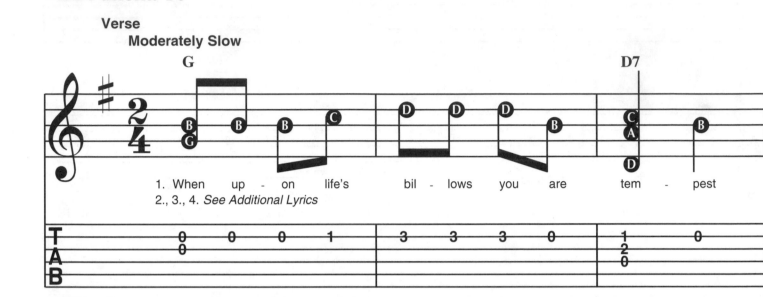

1. When up - on life's bil - lows you are tem - pest
2., 3., 4. *See Additional Lyrics*

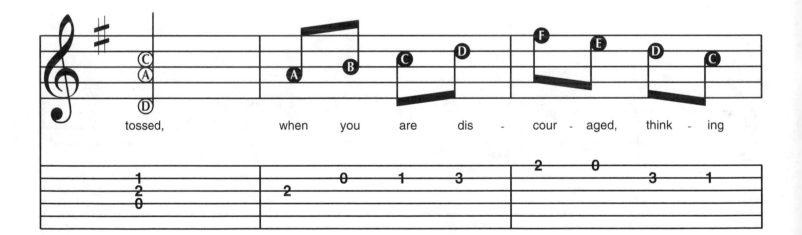

tossed, when you are dis - cour - aged, think - ing

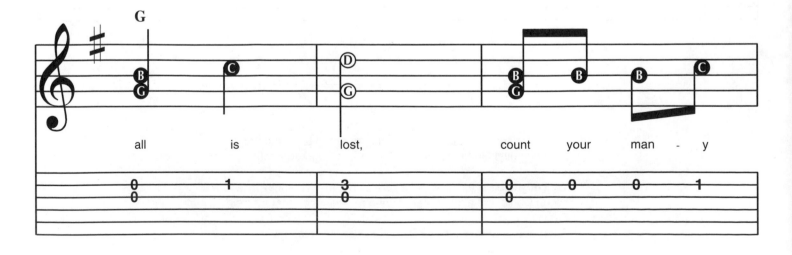

all is lost, count your man - y

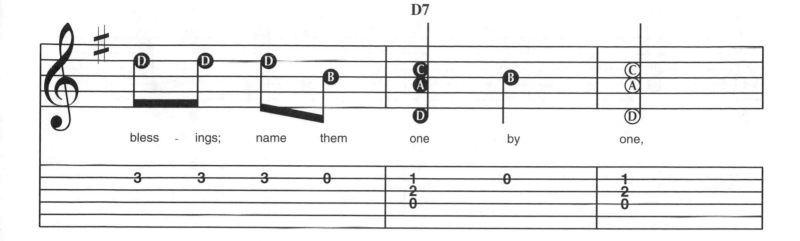

bless - ings; name them one by one,

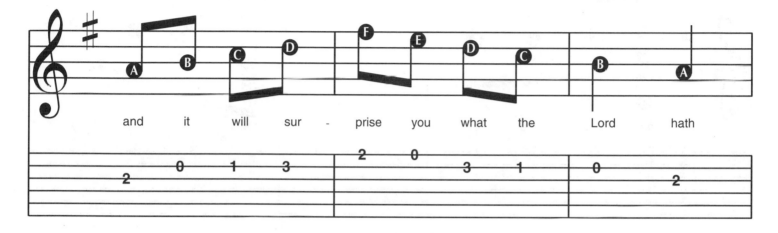

and it will sur - prise you what the Lord hath

Chorus

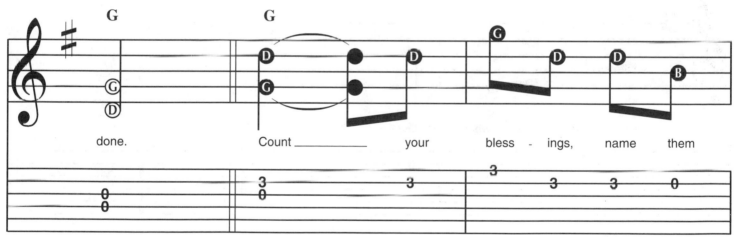

done. Count _____ your bless - ings, name them

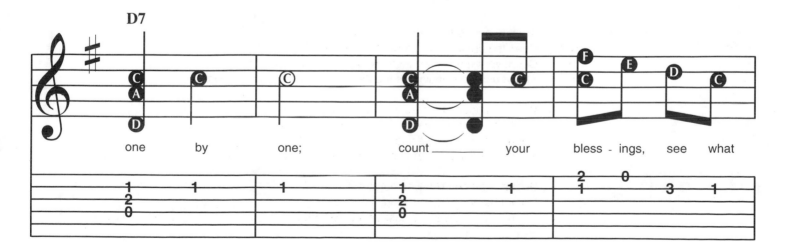

one by one; count _____ your bless - ings, see what

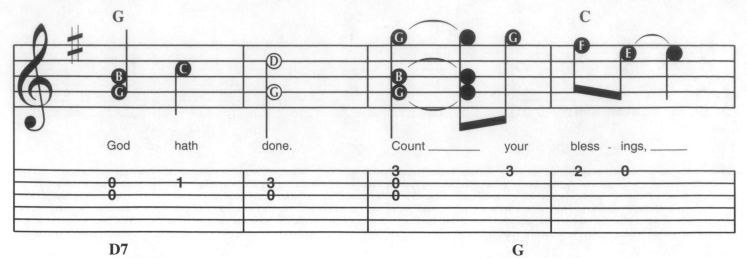

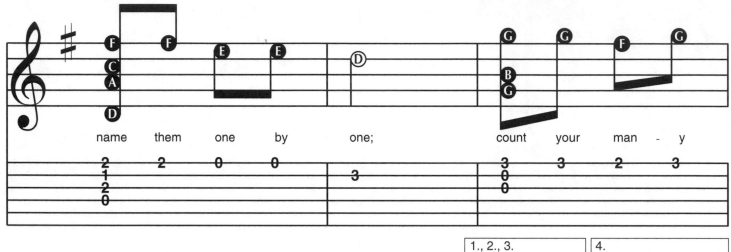

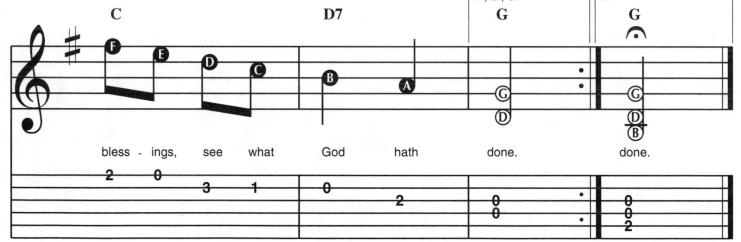

Additional Lyrics

2. Are you ever burdened with a load of care?
   Does the cross seem heavy you are called to bear?
   Count your many blessings; ev'ry doubt will fly,
   And you will be singing as the days go by.

3. When you look at others with their lands of gold,
   Think that Christ has promised you His wealth untold;
   Count your many blessings; money cannot buy
   Your reward in heaven nor your home on high.

4. So amid the conflict, whether great or small,
   Do not be discouraged; God is over all.
   Count your many blessings; angels will attend,
   Help and comfort give you to your journey's end.

Do Lord

Traditional

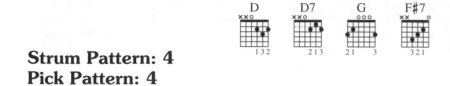

Strum Pattern: 4
Pick Pattern: 4

Chorus
Moderately Slow

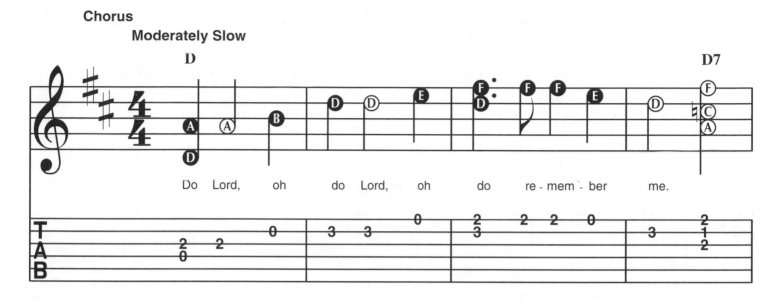

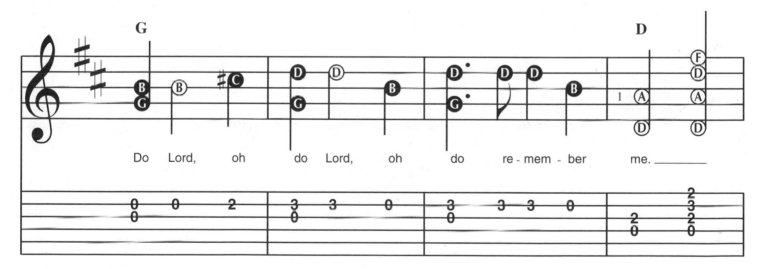

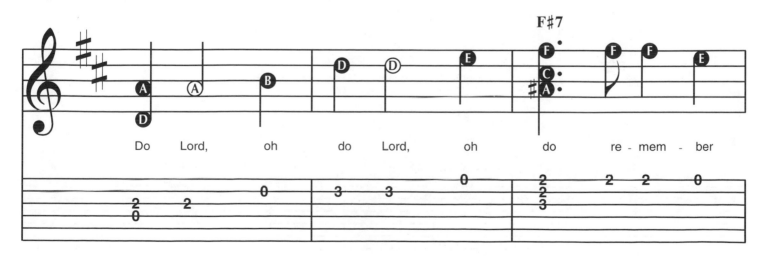

Bm   **D**   **A7**   **D**

me, _____ way be - yond _____ the blue. _____

Verse

G   **A7**   **D**

1. I've got a home in Glo - ry - land that
2. *See Additional Lyrics*

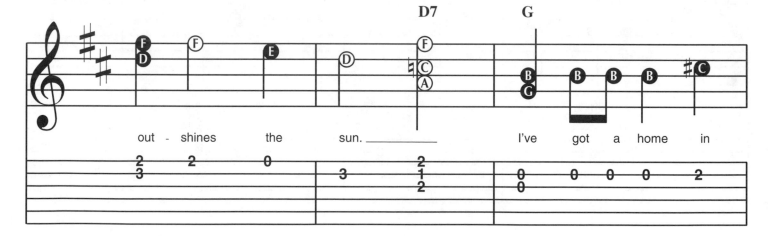

D7   **G**

out - shines the sun. _____ I've got a home in

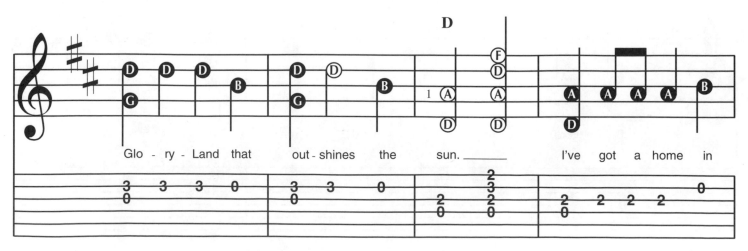

D

Glo - ry - Land that out - shines the sun. _____ I've got a home in

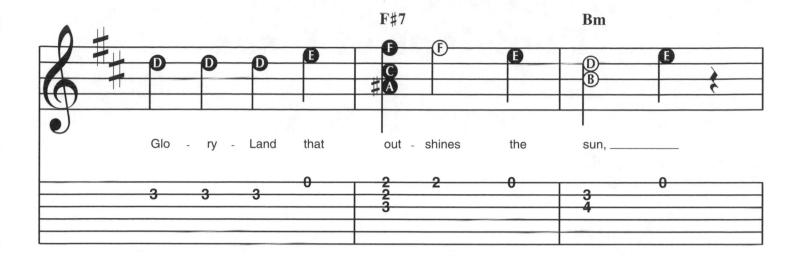

Glo - ry - Land that out - shines the sun, _____

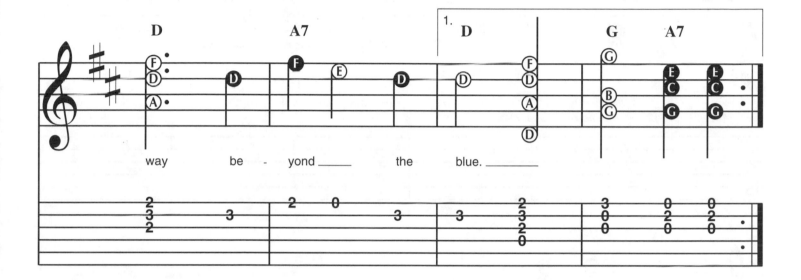

way be - yond _____ the blue. _____

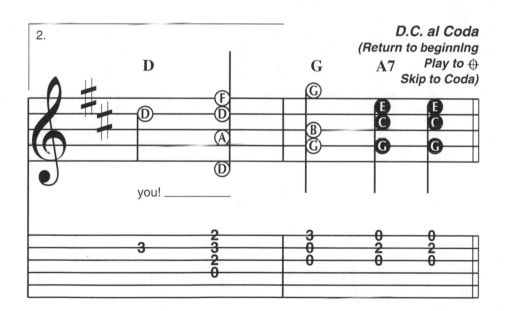

you! _____

D.C. al Coda
*(Return to beginning
Play to ⊕
Skip to Coda)*

⊕ *Coda*

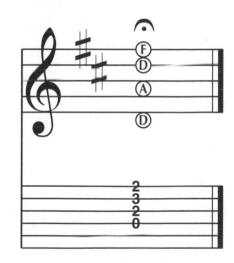

Additional Lyrics

2. I took Jesus as my Savior, you take Him too.
I took Jesus as my Savior, you take Him too.
I took Jesus as my Savior, you take Him too.
While He's calling you!

Footsteps of Jesus

Words by Mary B. C. Slade
Music by Asa B. Everett

Strum Pattern: 2, 4
Pick Pattern: 1, 3

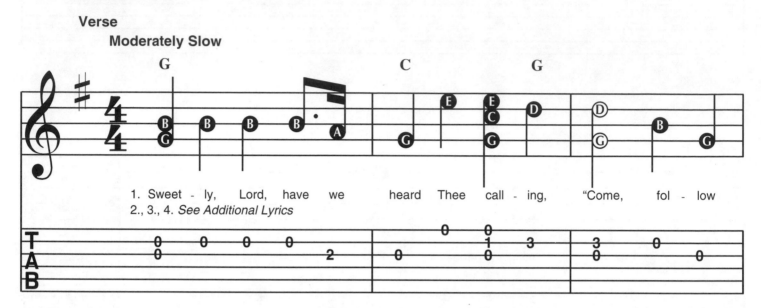

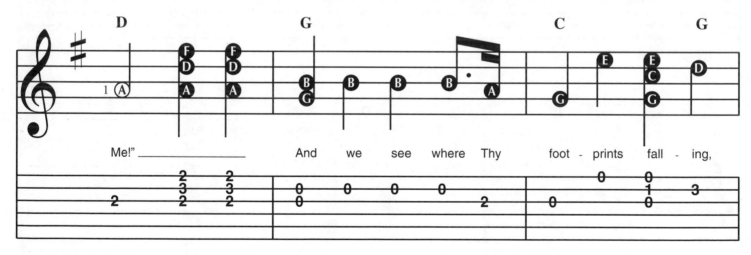

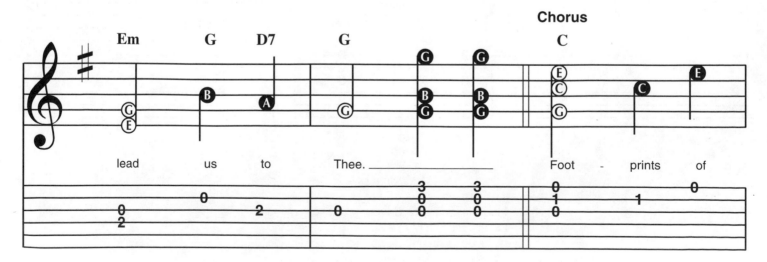

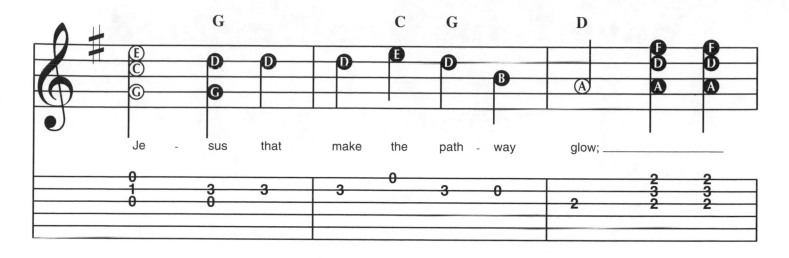

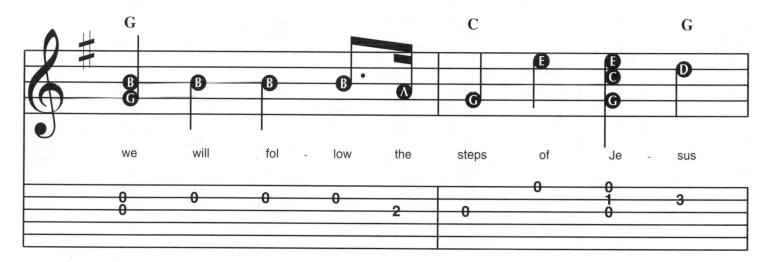

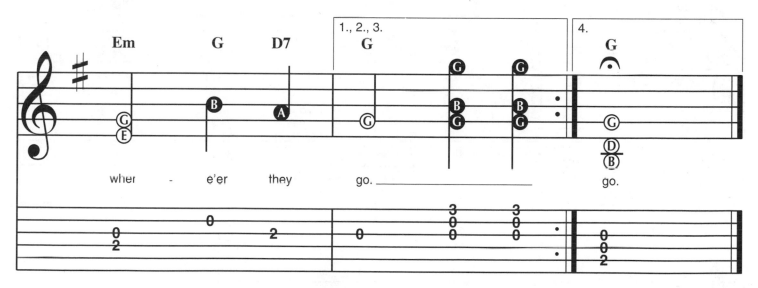

Additional Lyrics

2. Tho' they lead o'er the cold, dark mountains, seeking His sheep,
   Or along by Siloam's fountains, helping the weak.

3. If they lead thro' the temple holy, preaching the Word,
   Or in homes of the poor and lowly, serving the Lord.

4. Then at last, when on high He sees us, our journey done,
   We will rest where the steps of Jesus and at His throne.

Have Thine Own Way Lord

Words by Adelaide Pollard
Music by George Stebbins

Strum Pattern: 8
Pick Pattern: 8

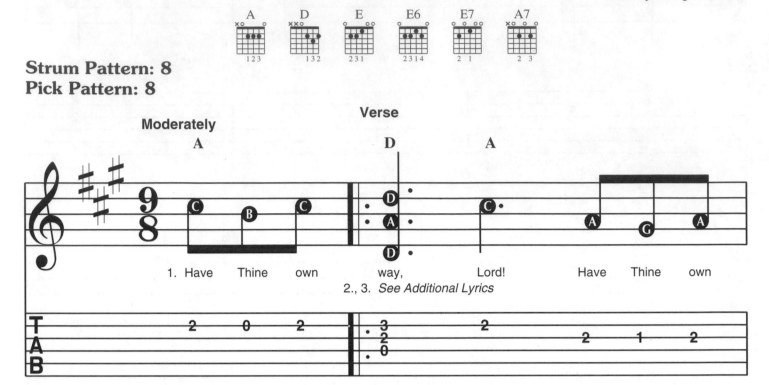

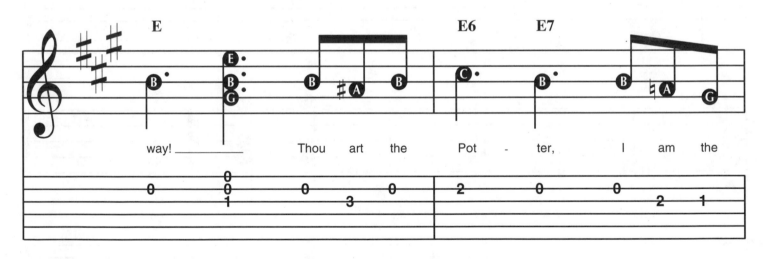

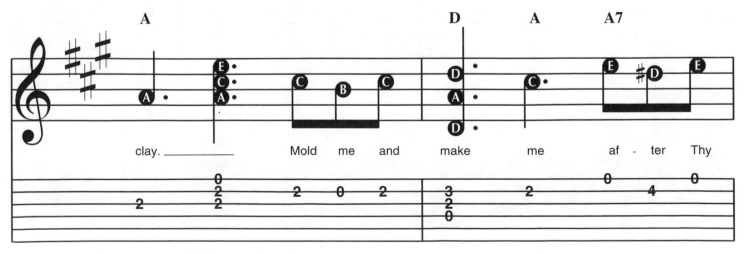

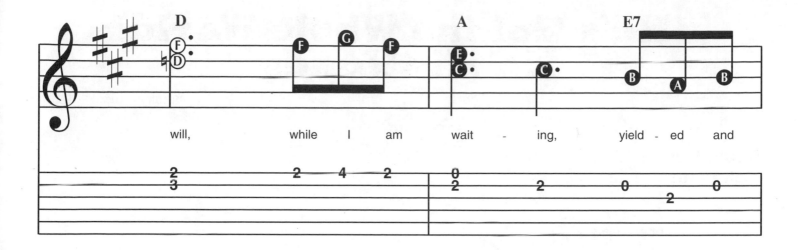

will, while I am wait - ing, yield - ed and

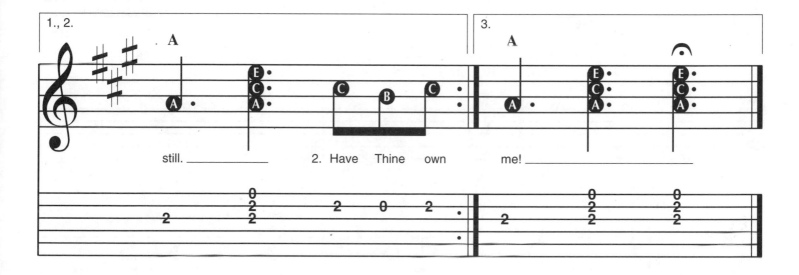

still. _____ 2. Have Thine own me! _____

Additional Lyrics

2. Have Thine own way, Lord! Have Thine own way!
   Search me and try me, Master, today!
   Whiter than snow, Lord, wash me just now,
   As in Thy presence humbly I bow.

3. Have Thine own way, Lord! Have Thine own way!
   Hold o'er my being absolute sway!
   Fill with Thy spirit till all shall see
   Christ only, always, living in me!

He's Got the Whole World in His Hands

African-American Folksong

Strum Pattern: 3, 4
Pick Pattern: 1, 3

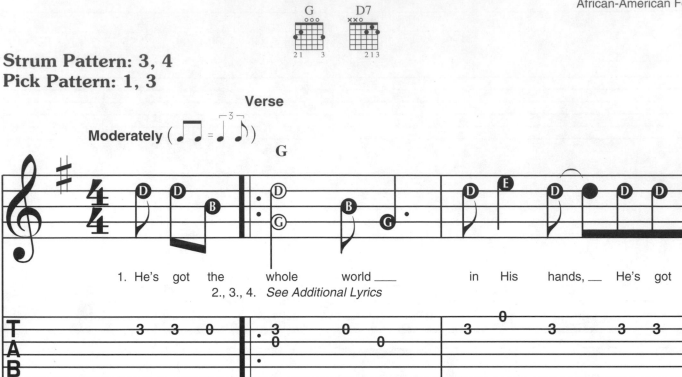

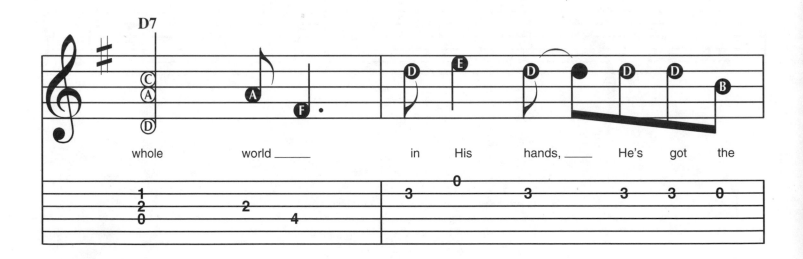

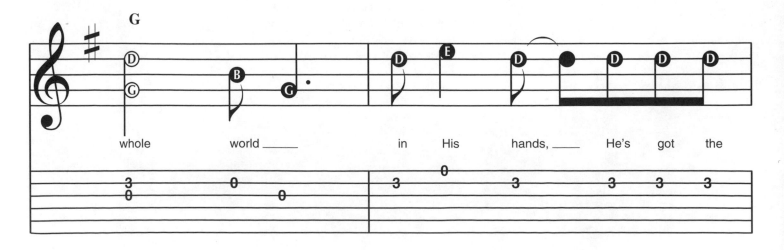

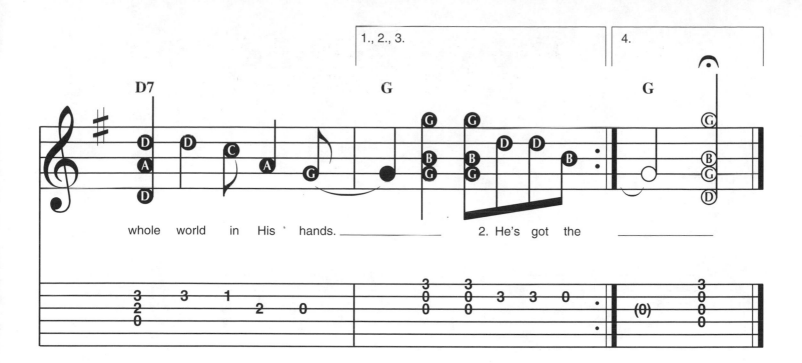

whole world in His hands. _____ 2. He's got the _____

Additional Lyrics

2. He's got the wind and the rain in His hands,
   He's got the wind and the rain in His hands,
   He's got the wind and the rain in His hands,
   He's got the whole world in His hands.

3. He's got the tiny little baby in His hands,
   He's got the tiny little baby in His hands,
   He's got the tiny little baby in His hands,
   He's got the whole world in His hands.

4. He's got you and me, brother, in His hands,
   He's got you and me, sister, in His hands,
   He's got you and me, brother, in His hands,
   He's got the whole world in His hands.

Higher Ground

Words by Johnson Oatman, Jr.
Music by Charles H. Gabriel

Strum Pattern: 8
Pick Pattern: 8

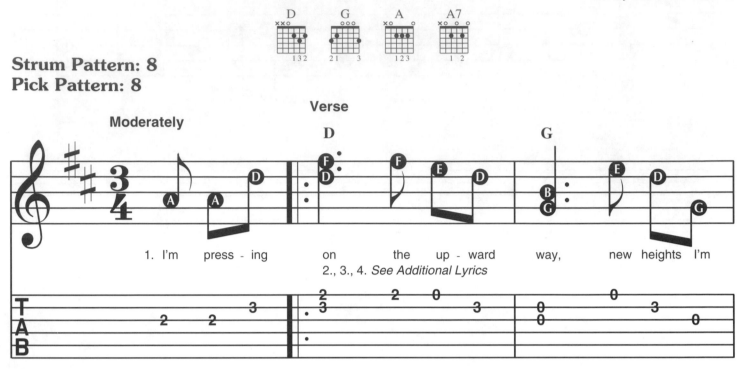

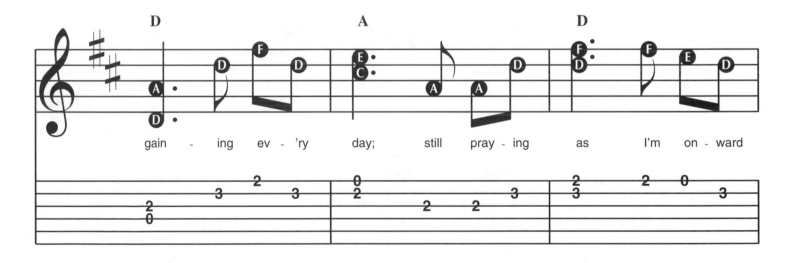

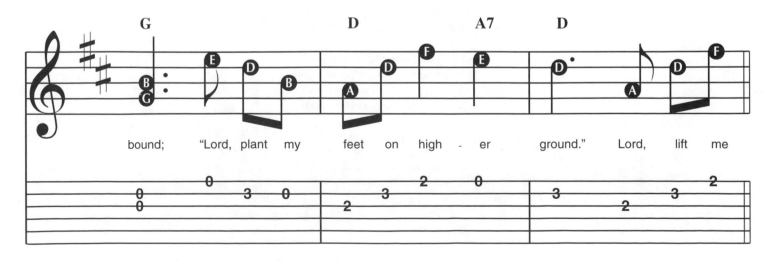

Chorus

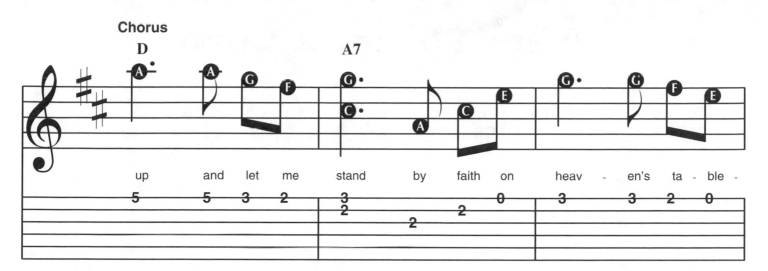

up and let me stand by faith on heav - en's ta - ble -

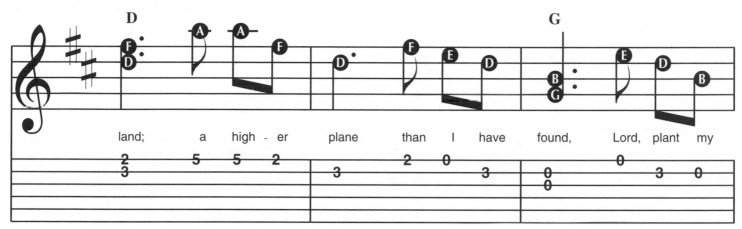

land; a high - er plane than I have found, Lord, plant my

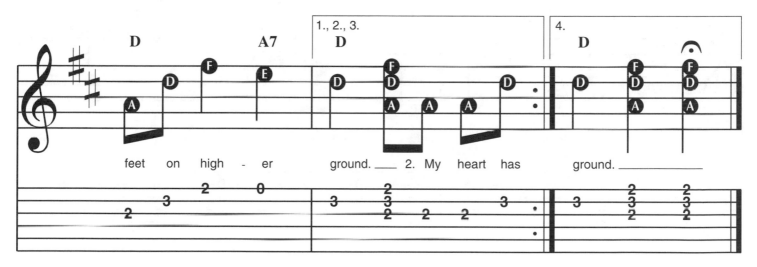

feet on high - er ground. ___ 2. My heart has ground. _____

Additional Lyrics

2. My heart has no desire to stay
   Where doubts arise and fears dismay;
   Tho' some may dwell where these abound,
   My prayer, my aim, is higher ground.

3. I want to live above the world,
   Tho' Satan's darts at me are hurled;
   For faith has caught the joyful sound,
   The song of saints on higher ground.

4. I want to scale the utmost height
   And catch a gleam of glory bright;
   But still I'll pray till heav'n I've found,
   "Lord, lead me on to higher ground."

I Am Thine, O Lord

Text by Fanny J. Crosby
Music by William H. Doane

Strum Pattern: 4
Pick Pattern: 4

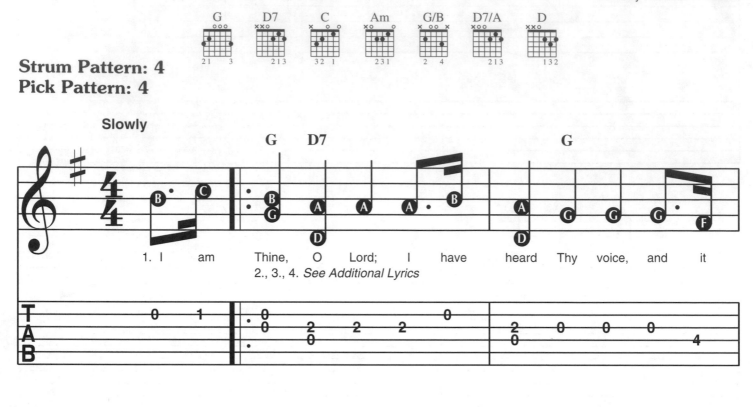

Slowly

1. I am Thine, O Lord; I have heard Thy voice, and it
2., 3., 4. *See Additional Lyrics*

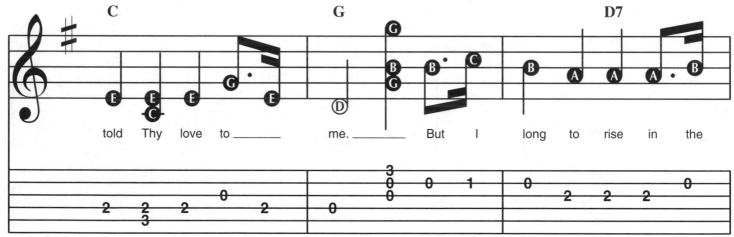

told Thy love to _____ me. _____ But I long to rise in the

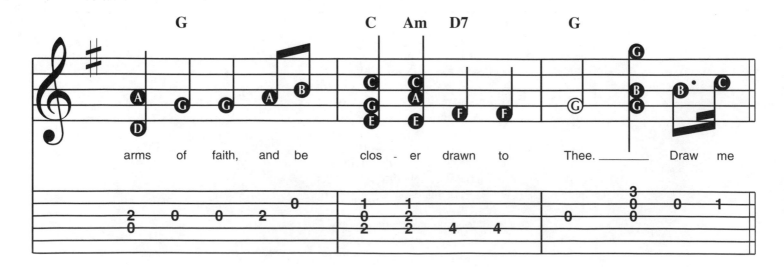

arms of faith, and be clos- er drawn to Thee. _____ Draw me

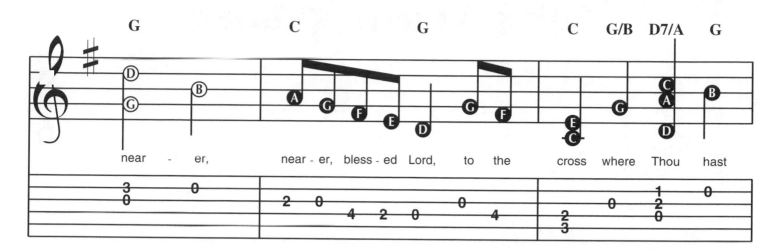

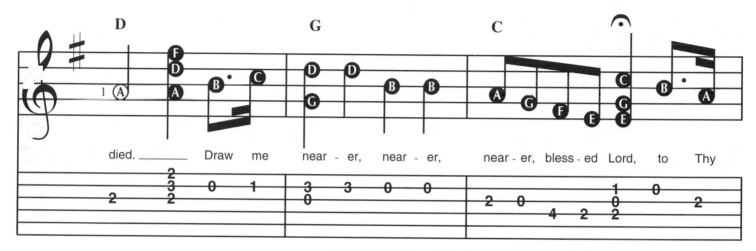

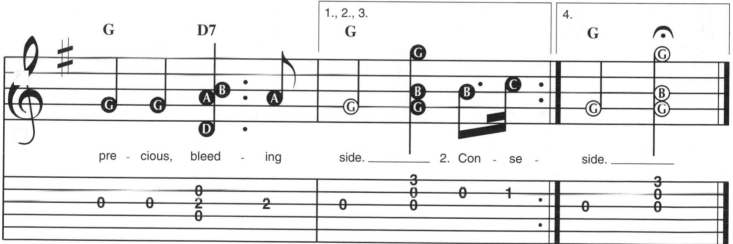

Additional Lyrics

2. Consecrate me now to Thy service, Lord,
   By the pow'r of grace divine.
   Let my soul look up with a steadfast hope,
   And my will be lost in Thine.

3. O the pure delight of a single hour
   That before Thy throne I spend,
   When I kneel in prayer and with Thee, my God,
   I commune as friend with friend!

4. There are depths of love that I cannot know
   Till I cross the narrow sea;
   There are heights of joy that I may not reach
   Till I rest in peace with Thee.

I Must Tell Jesus

Words and Music by
Elisha A. Hoffman

Strum Pattern: 7, 8
Pick Pattern: 7, 8

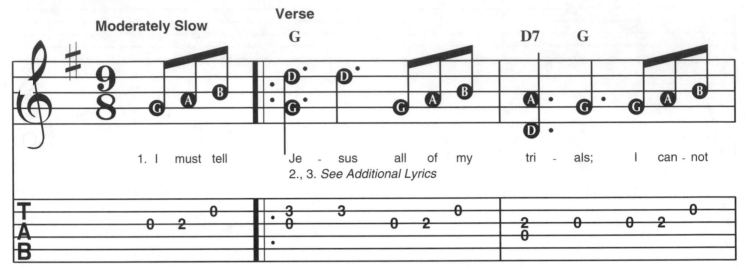

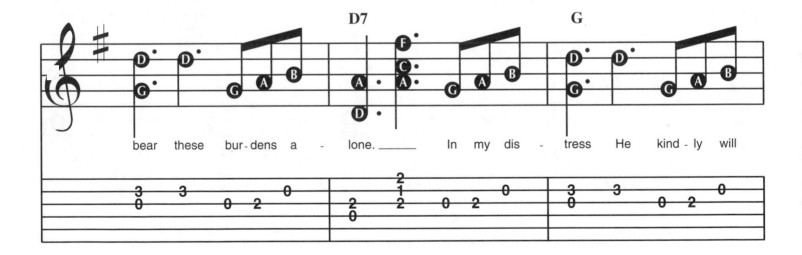

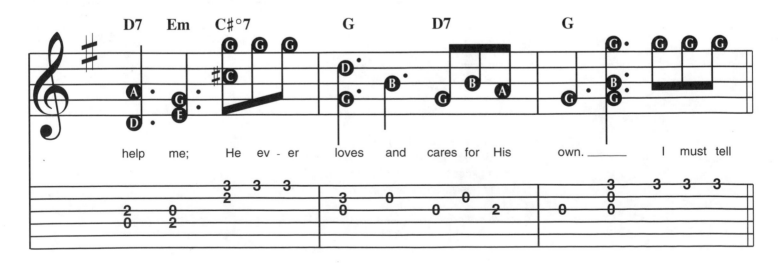

Chorus

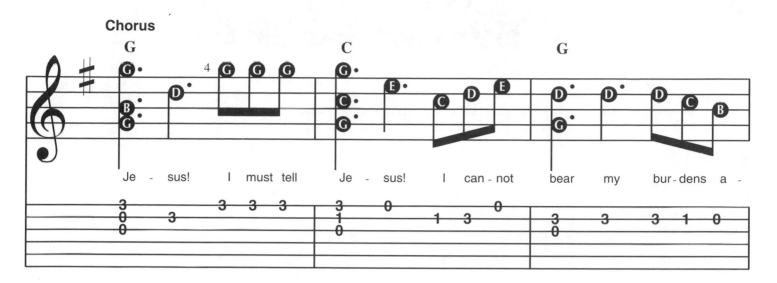

Je - sus! I must tell Je - sus! I can - not bear my bur - dens a -

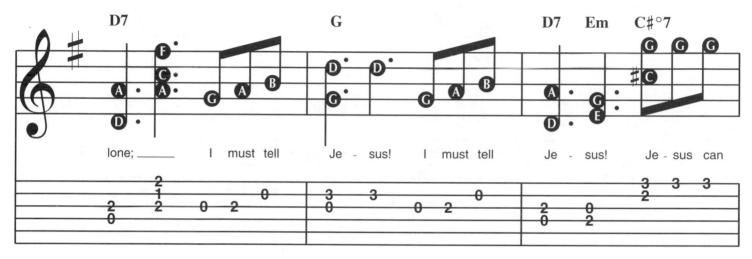

lone; _____ I must tell Je - sus! I must tell Je - sus! Je - sus can

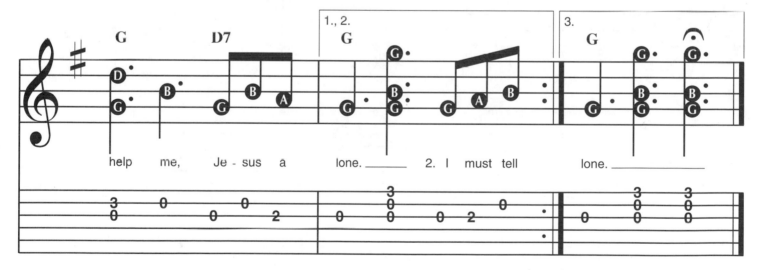

help me, Je - sus a - lone. _____ 2. I must tell lone. _____

Additional Lyrics

2. I must tell Jesus all of my troubles;
   He is a kind, compassionate Friend.
   If I but ask Him, He will deliver,
   Make of my troubles quickly an end.

3. O how the world to evil allures me!
   O how my heart is tempted to sin!
   I must tell Jesus, and He will help me
   Over the world the vict'ry to win.

I Surrender All

Words by J.W. Van Deventer
Music by W.S. Weeden

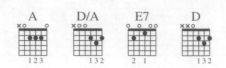

Strum Pattern: 3, 4
Pick Pattern: 2, 4

Verse
Moderately Slow

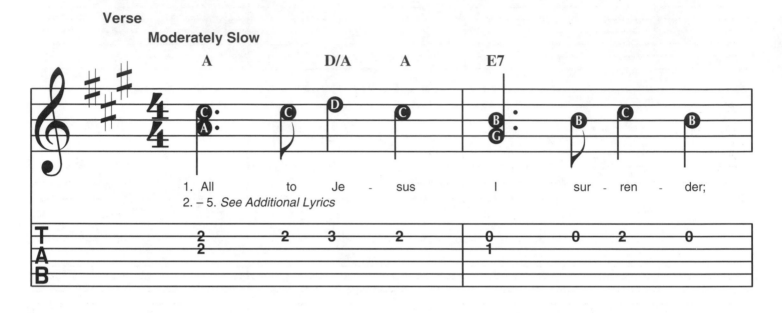

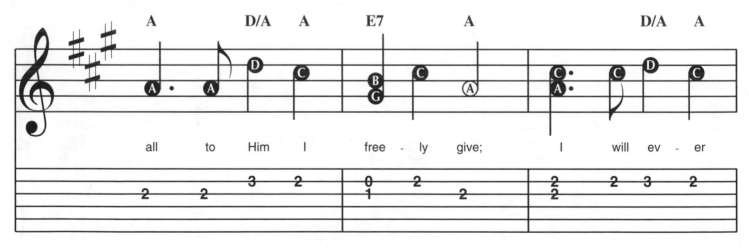

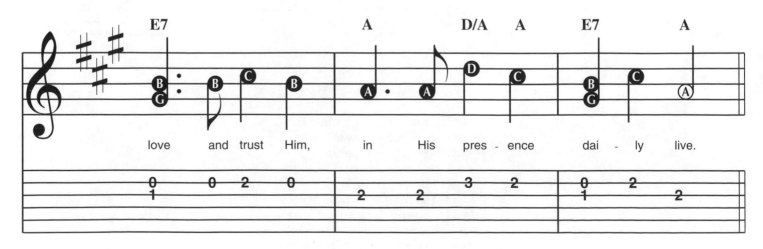

Chorus

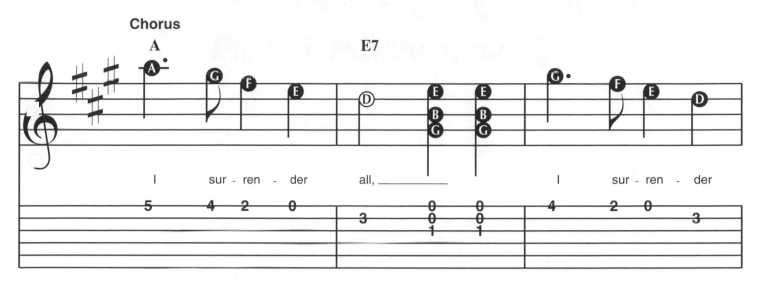

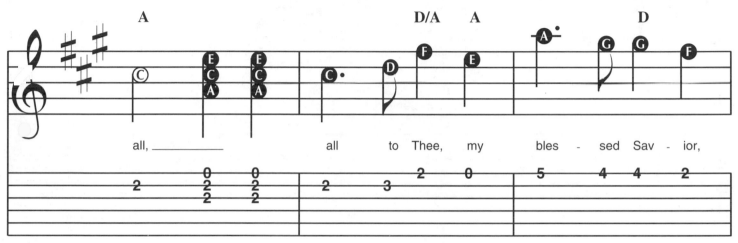

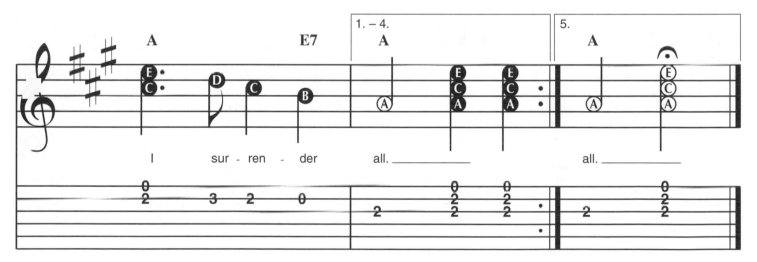

Additional Lyrics

2. All to Jesus I surrender; humbly at His feet I bow,
   Worldly pleasures all foresaken; take me, Jesus, take me now.

3. All to Jesus I surrender; make me, Savior, wholly Thine;
   Let me feel the Holy Spirit, truly know that Thou art mine.

4. All to Jesus I surrender; Lord, I give myself to Thee;
   Fill me with Thy love and power; let Thy blessing fall on me.

5. All to Jesus I surrender; now I feel the sacred flame.
   O the joy of full salvation! Glory, glory to His name!

Jesus Paid It All

Words and Music by H.M. Hall
and John T. Grape

Strum Pattern: 8
Pick Pattern: 8

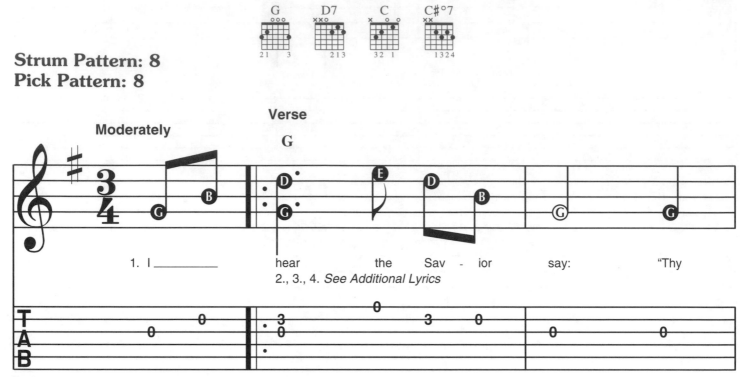

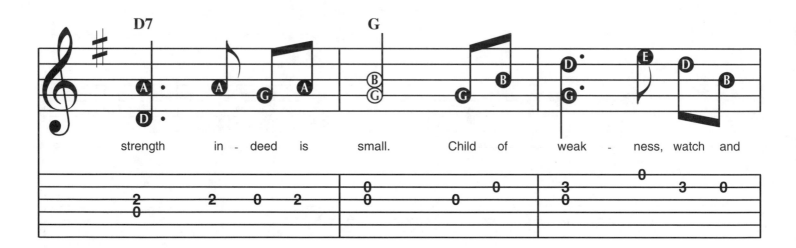

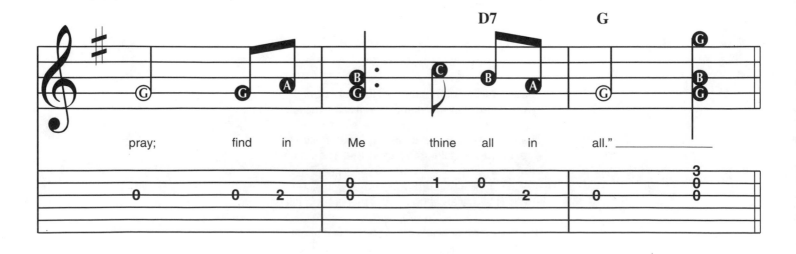

Chorus

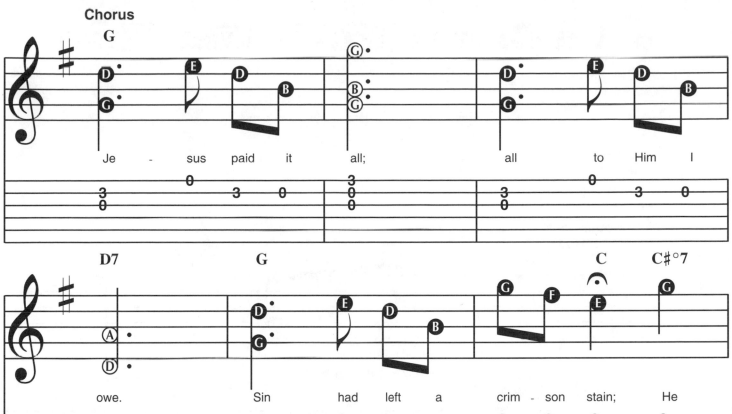

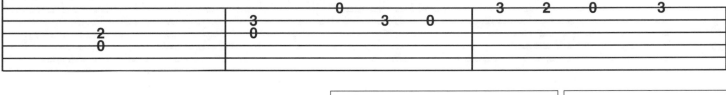

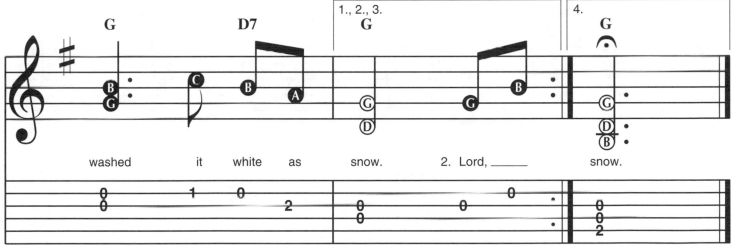

Additional Lyrics

2. Lord, now indeed I find
   Thy pow'r, and Thine alone
   Can change the leper's spots
   And melt the heart of stone.

3. For nothing good have I
   Whereby Thy grace to claim;
   I'll wash my garments white
   In the blood of Calv'ry's Lamb.

4. And when before the throne
   I stand in Him complete,
   "Jesus dies my soul to save,"
   My lips shall still repeat.

Just a Closer Walk With Thee

Traditional
Arranged by Kenneth Morris

Strum Pattern: 4
Pick Pattern: 5

Chorus

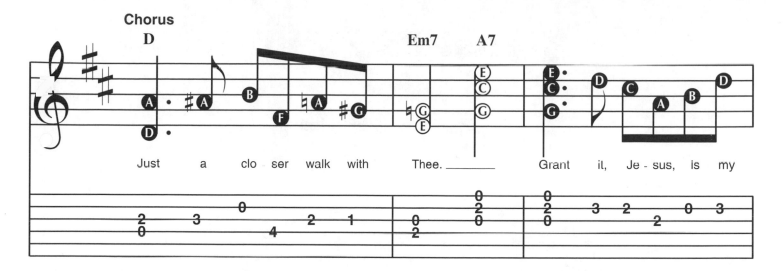

Just a clo- ser walk with Thee. _____ Grant it, Je- sus, is my

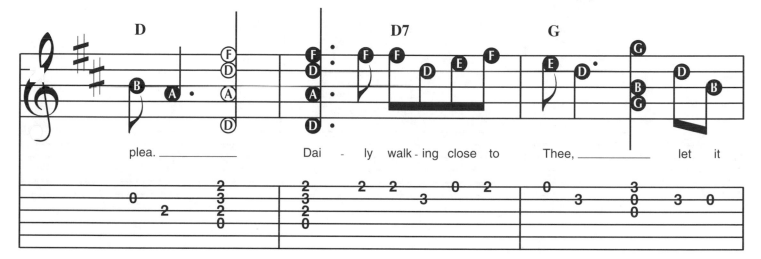

plea. _____ Dai- ly walk- ing close to Thee, _____ let it

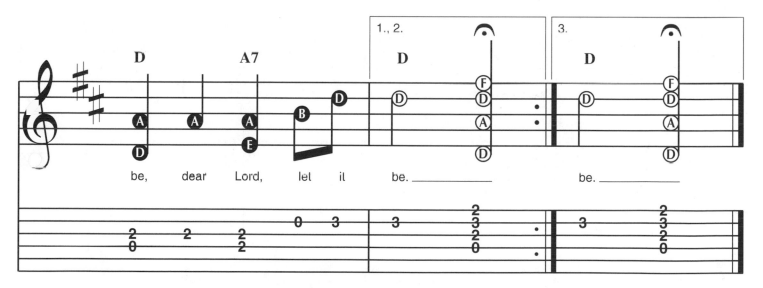

be, dear Lord, let it be. _____ be. _____

Additional Lyrics

2. Through this world of toil and snares,
   If I falter, Lord, who cares?
   Who with me my burden share?
   None but Thee, dear Lord, none but Thee.

3. When my feeble life is o'er,
   Time for me will be no more;
   Guide me gently, safely o'er
   To Thy kingdom shore, to Thy shore.

Just As I Am

Words by Charlotte Elliott
Music by William Bradbury

Strum Pattern: 8
Pick Pattern: 8

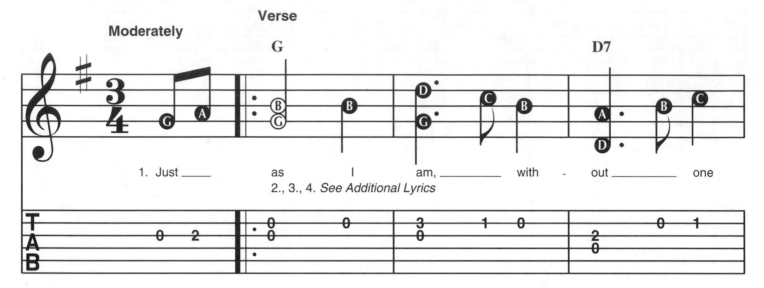

Moderately

Verse

1. Just _____ as I am, _____ with - out _____ one
2., 3., 4. *See Additional Lyrics*

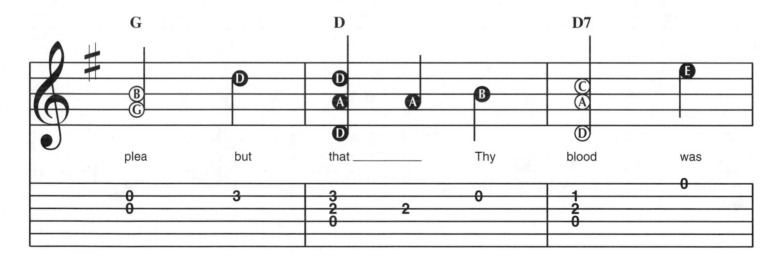

plea but that _____ Thy blood was

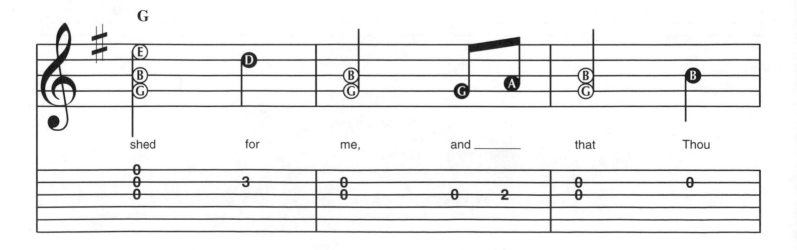

shed for me, and _____ that Thou

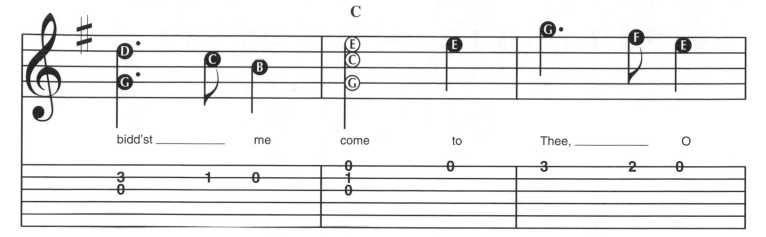

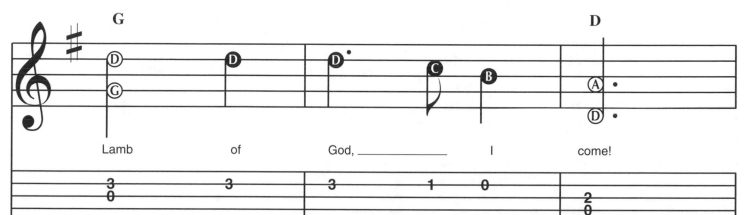

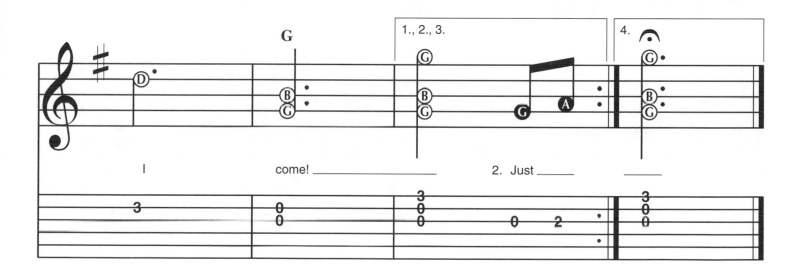

Additional Lyrics

2. Just as I am and waiting
   Not to rid my soul of one dark blot,
   To Thee whose blood can cleanse each spot,
   O Lamb of God, I come! I come!

3. Just as I am, though tossed about
   With many a conflict, many a doubt,
   Fightings and fears within, without,
   O Lamb of God, I come! I come!

4. Just as I am; Thou wilt receive,
   Wilt welcome, pardon, cleanse, relieve.
   Because Thy promise I believe,
   O Lamb of God, I come! I come!

Leaning on the Everlasting Arms

Words by Elisha A. Hoffman
Music by Anthony J. Showalter

Strum Pattern: 4
Pick Pattern: 5

Verse
Moderately Slow

1. What a fel - low - ship, what a joy di - vine,
2., 3. *See Additional Lyrics*

lean - ing on the ev - er - last - ing arms. What a bless - ed - ness,

what a peace is mine, lean - ing on the ev - er - last - ing arms.

Copyright © 2000 by HAL LEONARD CORPORATION
International Copyright Secured   All Rights Reserved

40

Additional Lyrics

2. O how sweet to walk in this pilgrim way,
   Leaning on the everlasting arms.
   O how bright the path grows from day to day,
   Leaning on the everlasting arms.

3. What have I to dread, what have I to fear,
   Leaning on the everlasting arms?
   I have blessed peace with my Lord so near,
   Leaning on the everlasting arms.

My Savior First of All

Words by Fanny J. Crosby
Music by John R. Sweney

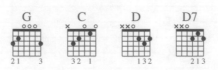

Strum Pattern: 4
Pick Pattern: 4

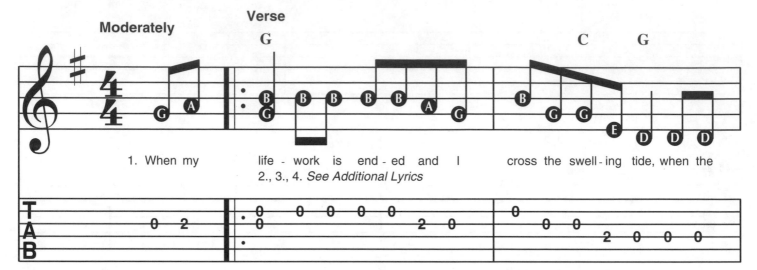

1. When my life-work is end-ed and I cross the swell-ing tide, when the
2., 3., 4. *See Additional Lyrics*

bright and glo-rious morn-ing I shall see;____ I shall know my Re-deem-er when I

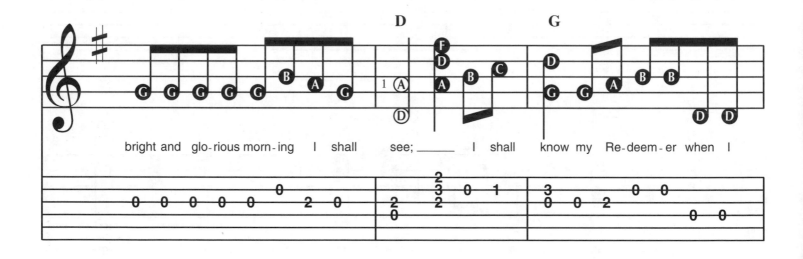

reach the oth-er side, and His smile will be the first to wel-come me.____ I shall

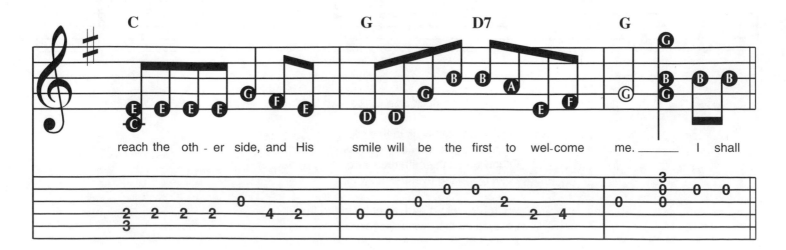

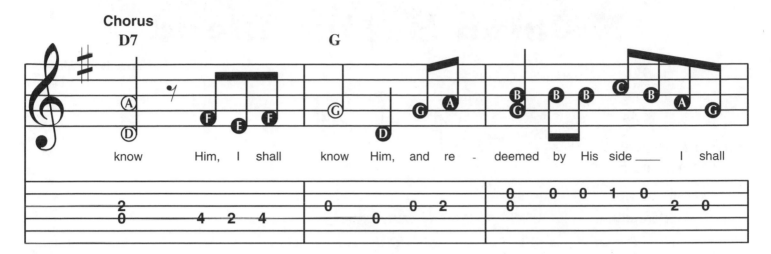

know Him, I shall know Him, and re - deemed by His side ___ I shall

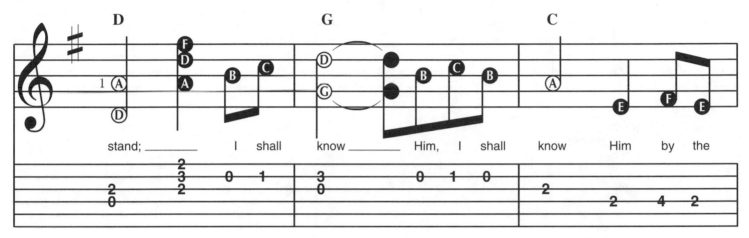

stand; _____ I shall know _____ Him, I shall know Him by the

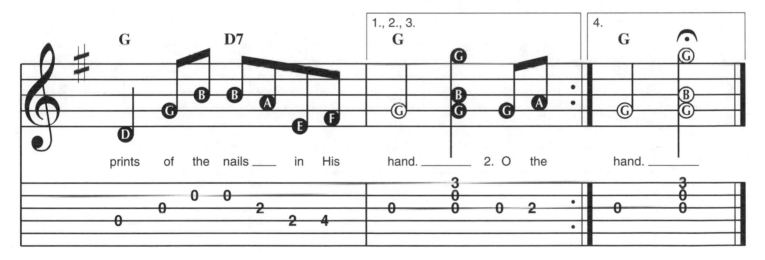

prints of the nails ___ in His hand. _____ 2. O the hand. _____

Additional Lyrics

2. O the soul-thrilling rapture when I view His blessed face
And the luster of His kindly beaming eye;
How my full heart will praise Him for the mercy, love and grace
That prepare for me a mansion in the sky.

3. O the dear ones in glory; how they beckon me to come,
And our parting at the river I recall;
To the sweet vales of Eden they will sing my welcome home,
But I long to meet my Savior first of all.

4. Through the gates to the city in a robe of spotless white,
He will lead me where no tears will ever fall;
In the glad song of ages I shall mingle with delight,
But I long to meet my Savior first of all.

Nothing But the Blood

Words and Music by
Robert Lowry

Strum Pattern: 4
Pick Pattern: 5

Verse
Moderately

1. What can wash a - way my sin?
2., 3., 4. *See Additional Lyrics*

Noth - ing but the blood of Je - sus; what can make me

whole a - gain? Noth - ing but the blood of Je - sus.

Additional Lyrics

2. For my pardon this I see,
   Nothing but the blood of Jesus;
   For my cleansing, this my plea,
   Nothing but the blood of Jesus.

3. Nothing can for sin atone,
   Nothing but the blood of Jesus;
   Naught of good that I have done,
   Nothing but the blood of Jesus.

4. This all my hope and peace,
   Nothing but the blood of Jesus;
   This is all my righteousness,
   Nothing but the blood of Jesus.

O Happy Day

Words by Rev. Philip Doddridge
Music by Edward F. Rimbault

Strum Pattern: 8
Pick Pattern: 8

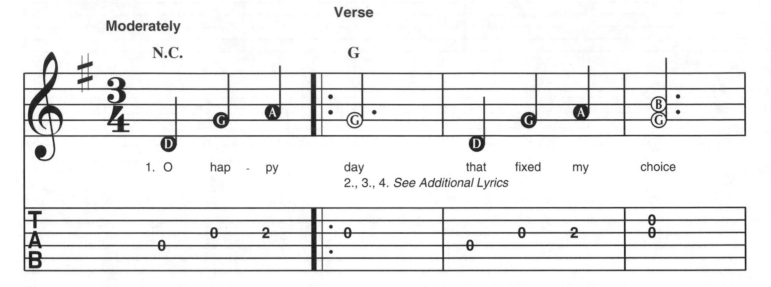

1. O hap - py day that fixed my choice
2., 3., 4. *See Additional Lyrics*

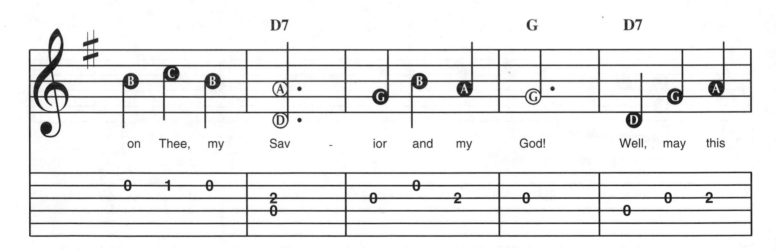

on Thee, my Sav - ior and my God! Well, may this

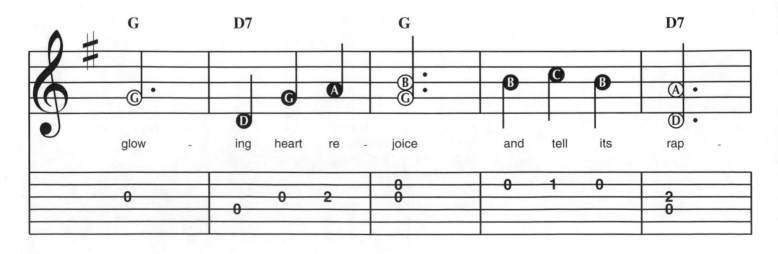

glow - ing heart re - joice and tell its rap -

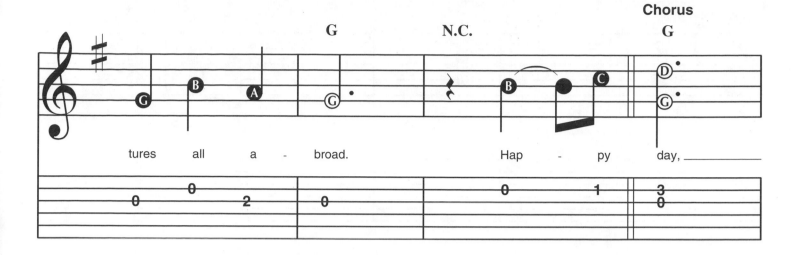

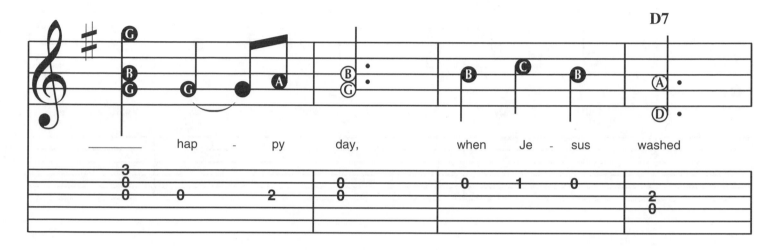

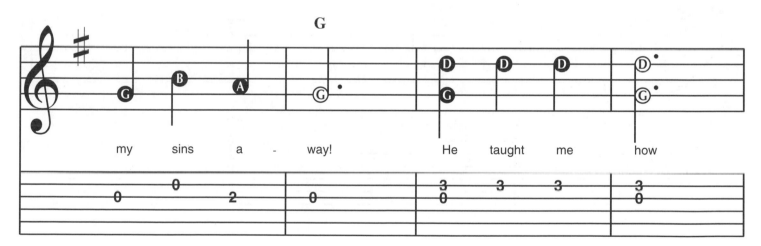

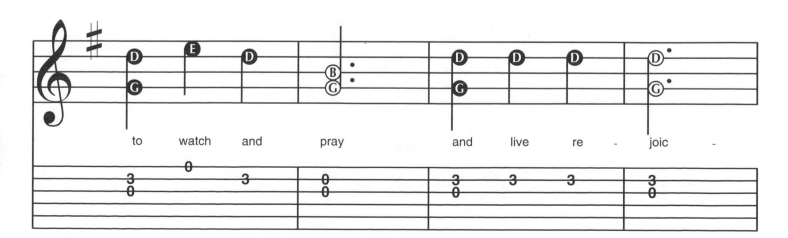

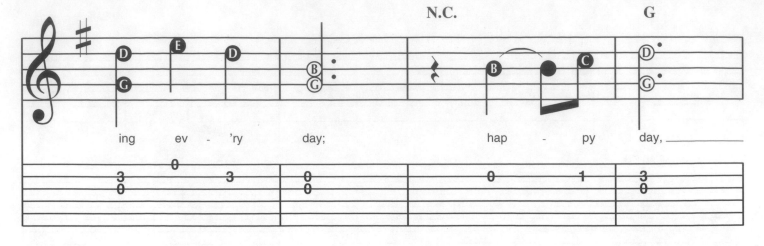

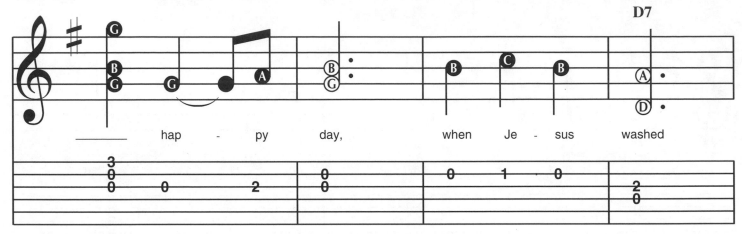

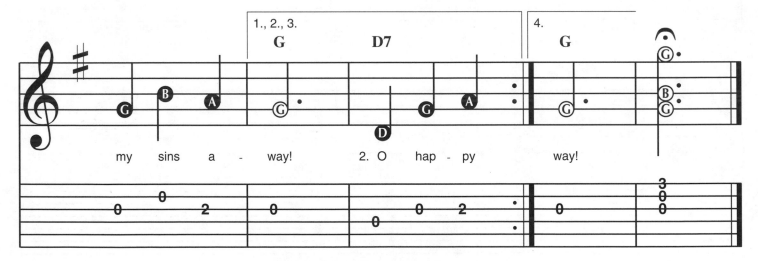

Additional Lyrics

2. O happy bond that seals my vows
   To Him who merits all my love!
   Let cheerful anthems fill His house,
   While to that sacred shrine I move.

3. 'Tis done, the great transactions done;
   I am my Lord's and He is mine;
   He drew me, and I followed on,
   Charmed to confess the voice divine.

4. Now rest, my long-divided heart,
   Fixed on the blissful center, rest,
   Nor ever from my Lord depart,
   With Him of ev'ry good possessed.

The Old Rugged Cross

Words and Music by
Rev. George Bennard

Strum Pattern: 9
Pick Pattern: 7

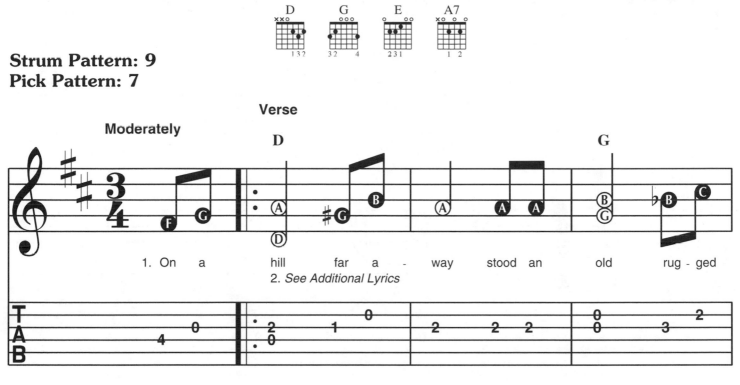

Verse

1. On a hill far a - way stood an old rug - ged
2. *See Additional Lyrics*

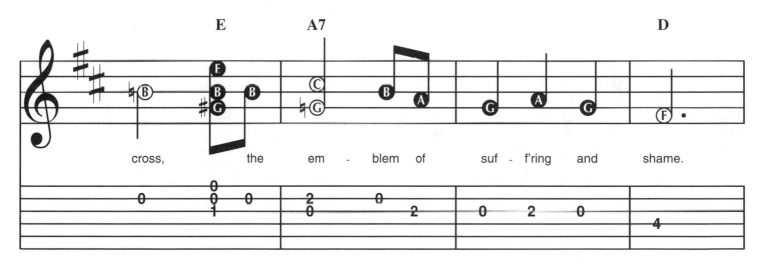

cross, the em - blem of suf - f'ring and shame.

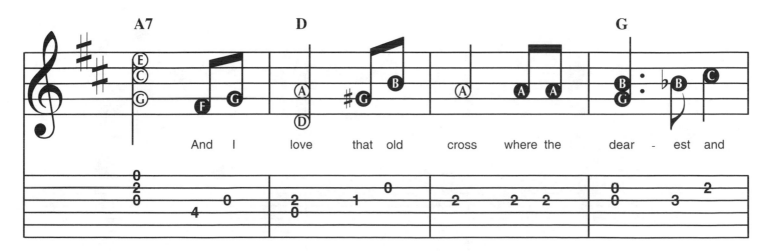

And I love that old cross where the dear - est and

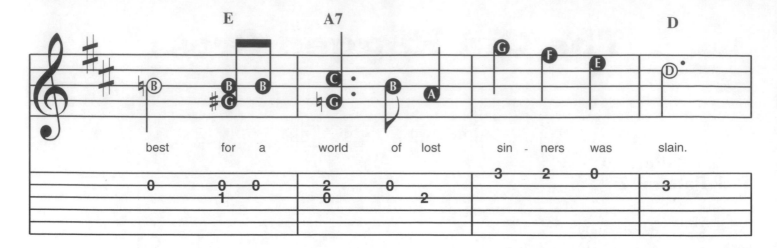

best for a world of lost sin - ners was slain.

Chorus

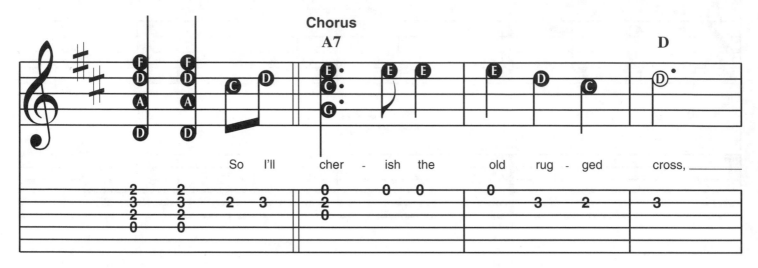

So I'll cher - ish the old rug - ged cross,

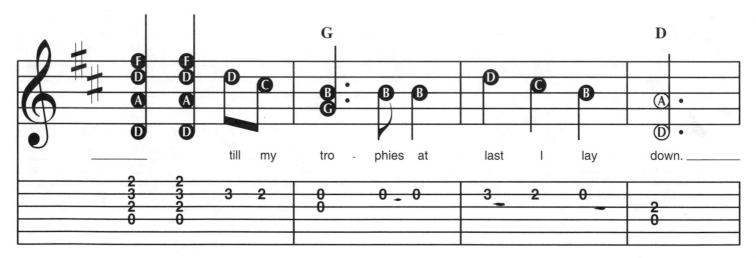

till my tro - phies at last I lay down.

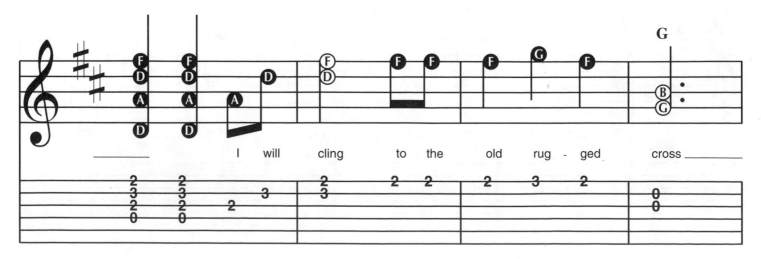

I will cling to the old rug - ged cross

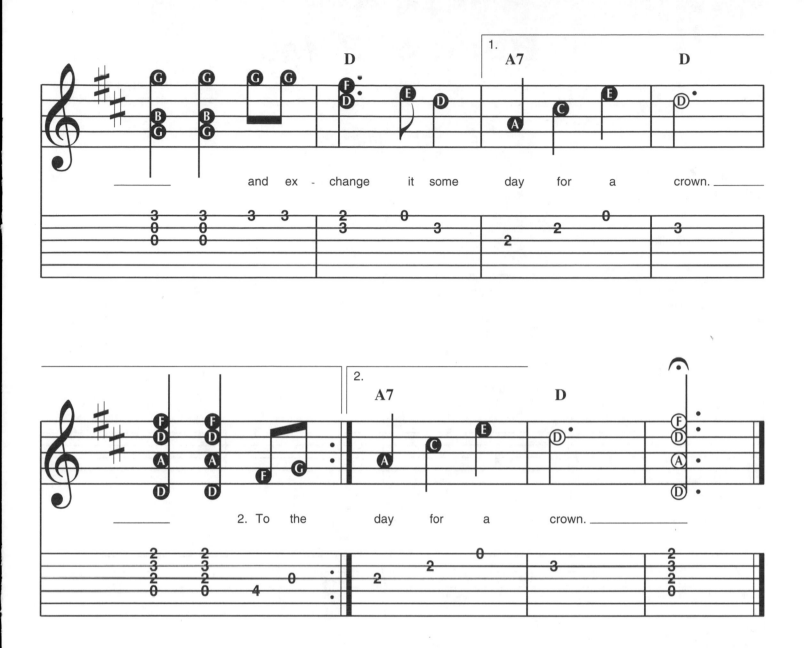

and ex - change it some day for a crown. _____

2. To the day for a crown. _____

Additional Lyrics

2. To the old rugged cross I will ever be true,
   Its shame and reproach gladly bear.
   Then He'll call me some day to my home far away,
   Where His glory forever I'll share.

Rock of Ages

Text by Augustus M. Toplady
Music by Thomas Hastings

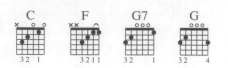

Strum Pattern: 8
Pick Pattern: 8

1. Rock of a - ges cleft for me, let me hide my - self in
2., 3. *See Additional Lyrics*

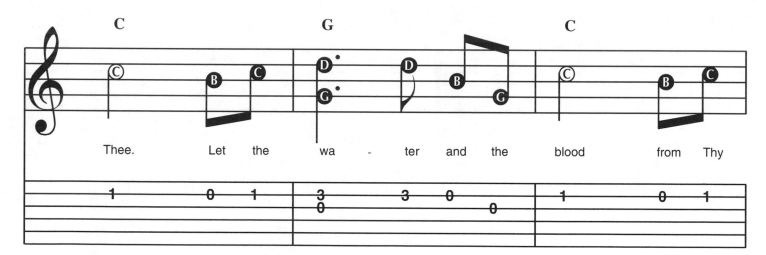

Thee. Let the wa - ter and the blood from Thy

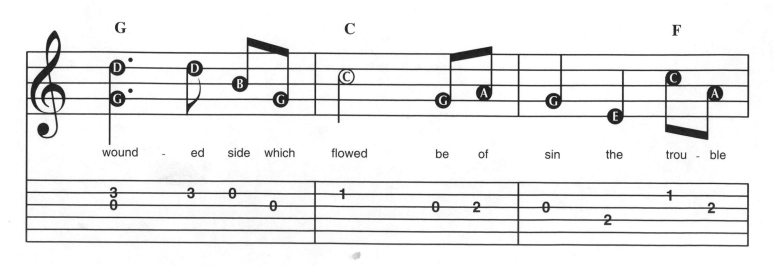

wound - ed side which flowed be of sin the trou - ble

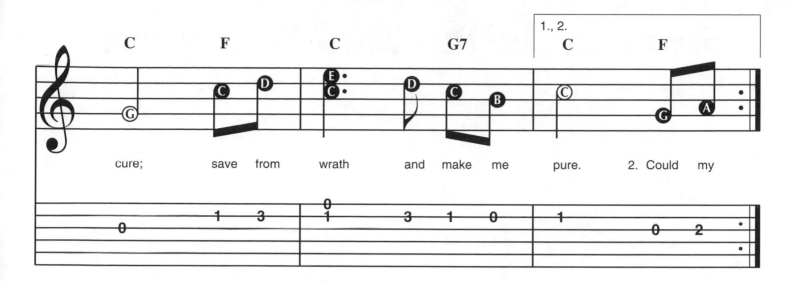

1., 2.

cure; save from wrath and make me pure. 2. Could my

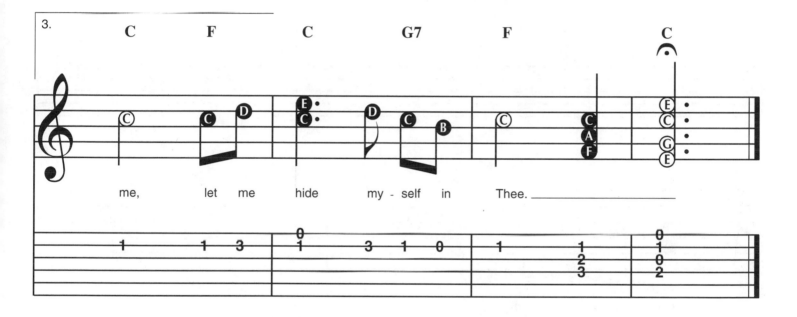

3.

me, let me hide my - self in Thee. _____

Additional Lyrics

2. Could my tears forever flow,
   Could my zeal no langour know?
   These for sin could not atone,
   Thou must save and Thou alone.
   In my hand no price I bring,
   Simply to Thy cross I cling.

3. While I draw this fleeting breath,
   When my eyes shall close in death.
   When I rise to worlds unknown,
   And behold Thee on Thy throne.
   Rock of ages cleft for me,
   Let me hide myself in Thee.

Standin' in the Need of Prayer

African-American Spiritual

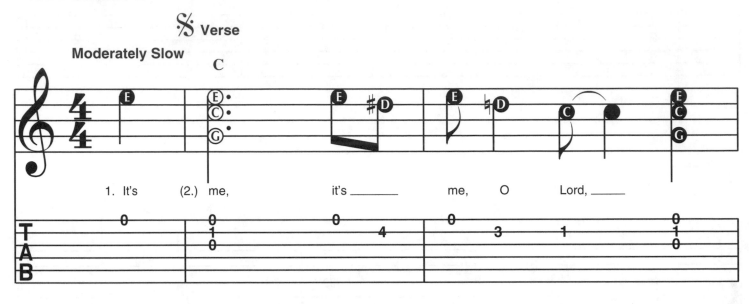

Strum Pattern: 4
Pick Pattern: 1

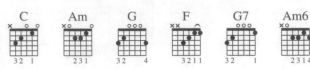

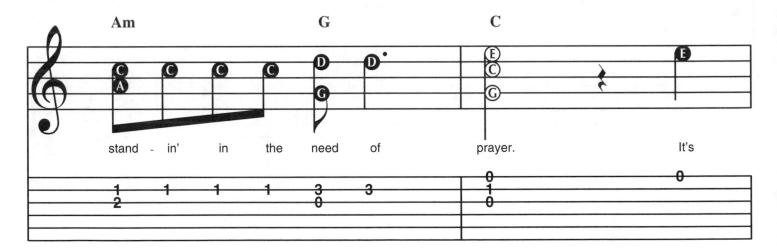

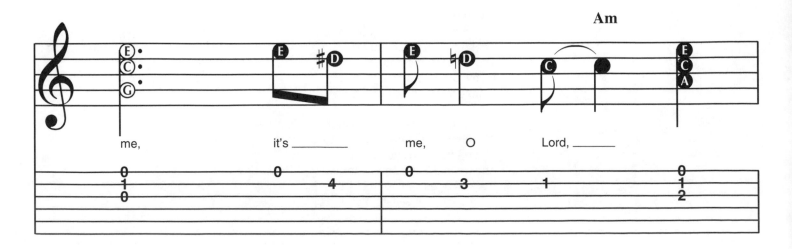

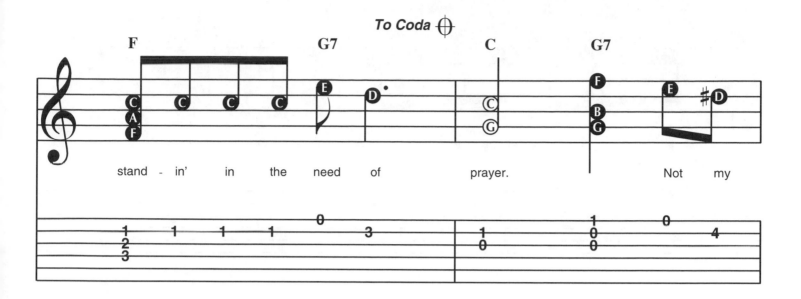

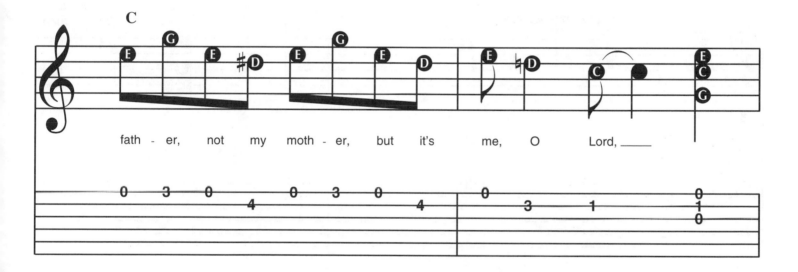

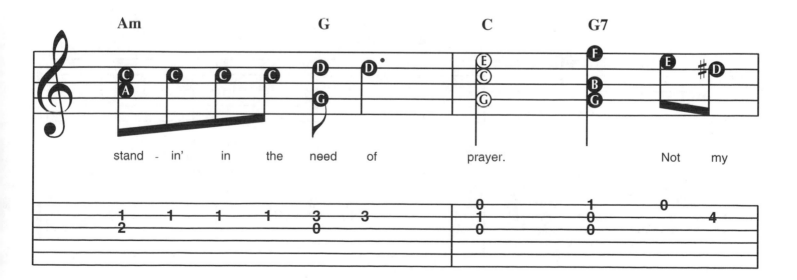

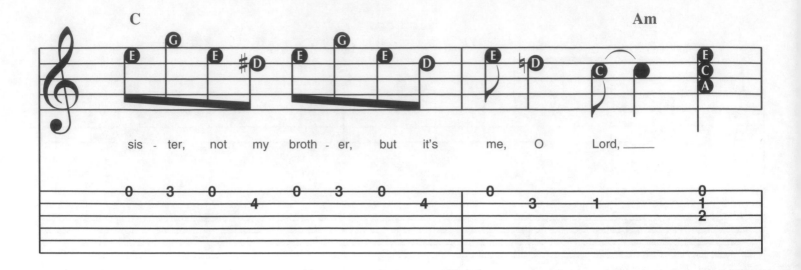

sis - ter, not my broth - er, but it's me, O Lord, _____

D.S. al Coda
(Return to 𝄋
Play to ⊕
Skip to Coda)

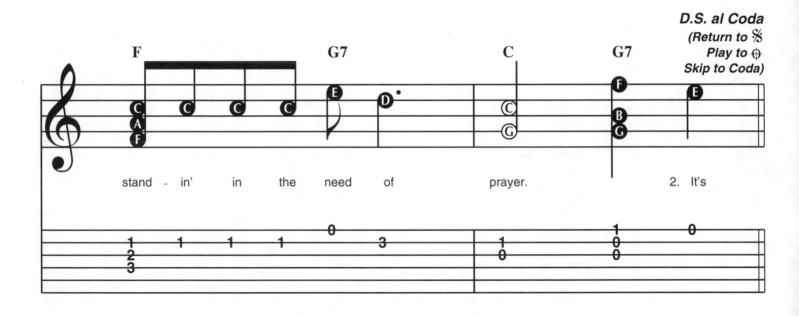

stand - in' in the need of prayer. 2. It's

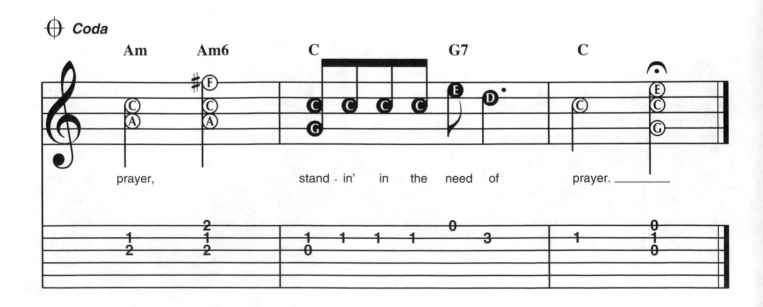

prayer, stand - in' in the need of prayer. _____

This Little Light of Mine

African-American Spiritual

C   F   G   G7

Strum Pattern: 2, 4
Pick Pattern: 5, 4

Chorus
Moderately

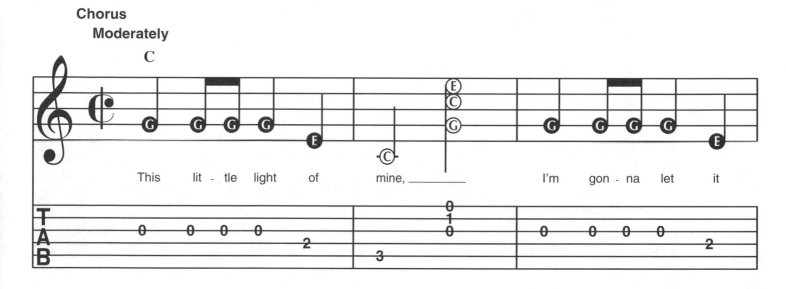

This lit - tle light of mine, _____ I'm gon - na let it

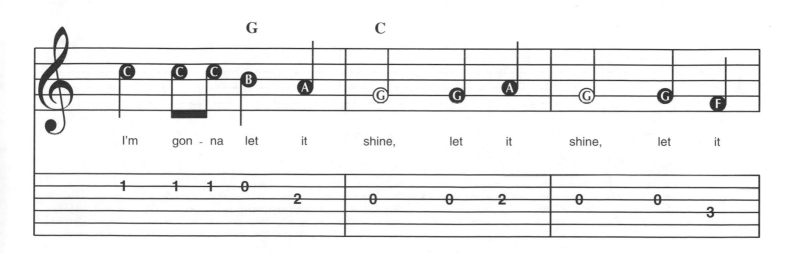

shine. _____ This lit - tle light of mine, _____

I'm gon - na let it shine, let it shine, let it

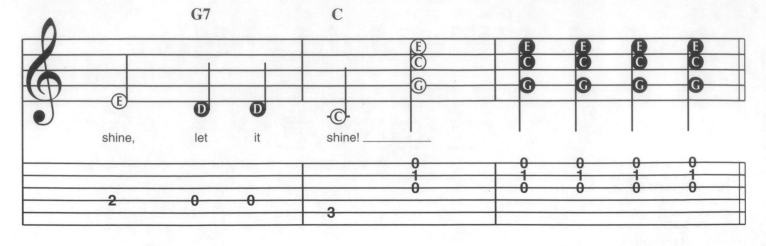

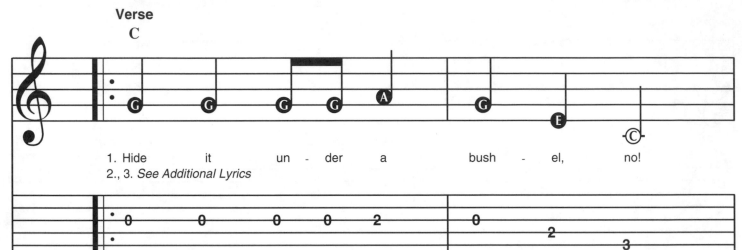

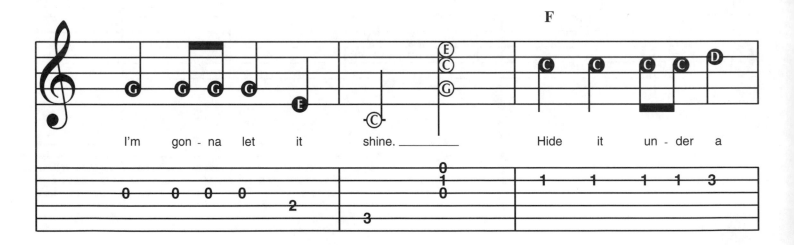

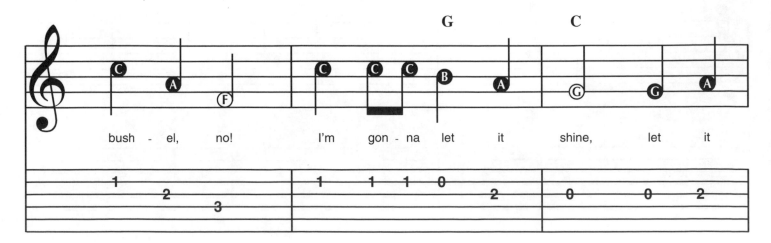

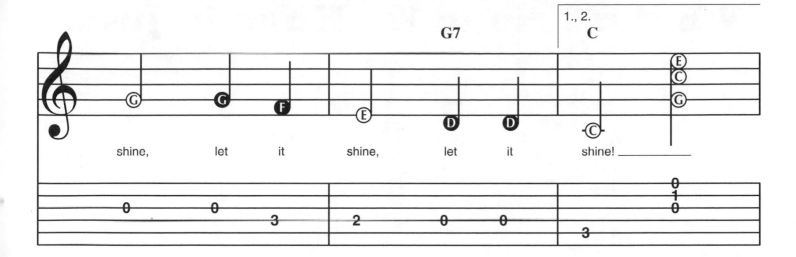

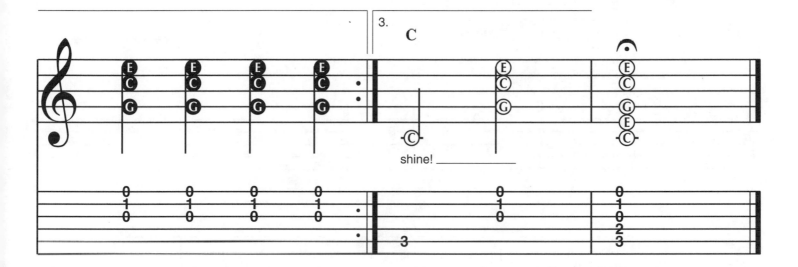

Additional Lyrics

2. Don't let Satan (blow) it out,
   I'm gonna let it shine.
   Don't let Satan (blow) it out,
   I'm gonna let it shine, let it shine,
   Let it shine, let it shine!

3. Let it shine till Jesus comes,
   I'm gonna let it shine.
   Let it shine till Jesus comes,
   I'm gonna let it shine, let it shine,
   Let it shine, let it shine!

What a Friend We Have in Jesus

Words by Joseph Scriven
Music by Charles C. Converse

Strum Pattern: 6
Pick Pattern: 4

1. What a friend we have in Je - sus, all our sins and griefs to
2., 3. *See Additional Lyrics*

bear. _____ What a priv - i - lege to car - ry

ev - 'ry - thing to God in prayer. _____

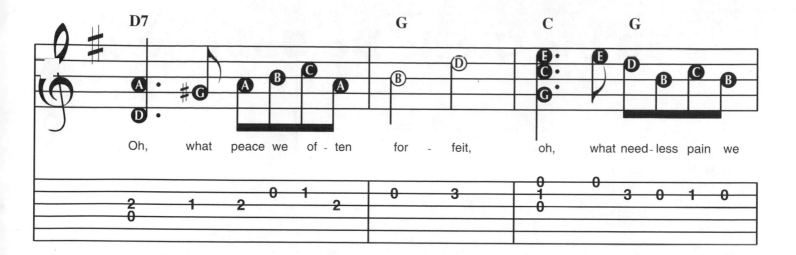

Oh, what peace we of-ten for-feit, oh, what need-less pain we

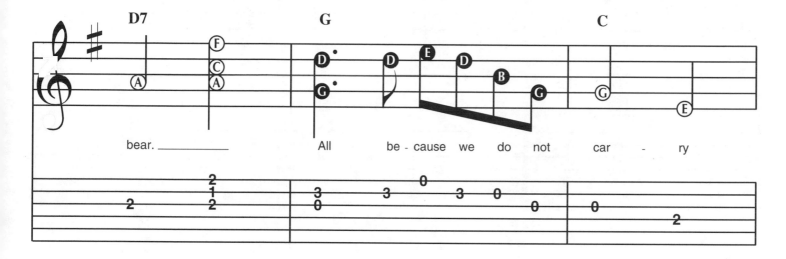

bear._____ All be-cause we do not car - ry

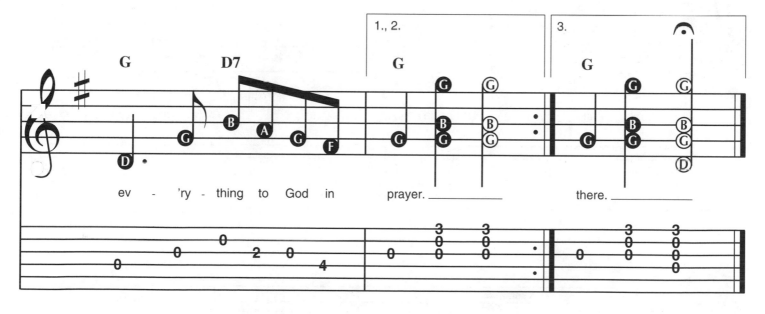

ev - 'ry - thing to God in prayer._____ there._____

Additional Lyrics

2. Have we trials and temptations,
   Is there troubles anywhere?
   We should never be discouraged;
   Take it to the Lord in prayer.
   Can we find a friend so faithful
   Who will all our sorrows share?
   Jesus knows our ev'ry weakness;
   Take it to the Lord in prayer.

3. Are we weak and heavy laden,
   Cumbered with a load of care?
   Precious Savior still our refuge;
   Take it to the Lord in prayer.
   Do thy friends despise, forsake thee?
   Take it to the Lord in prayer.
   In His arms He'll take and shield thee;
   Thou will find a solice there.

Will the Circle Be Unbroken

Words by Ada R. Habershon
Music by Charles H. Gabriel

G C D A7 D7

Strum Pattern: 3
Pick Pattern: 3

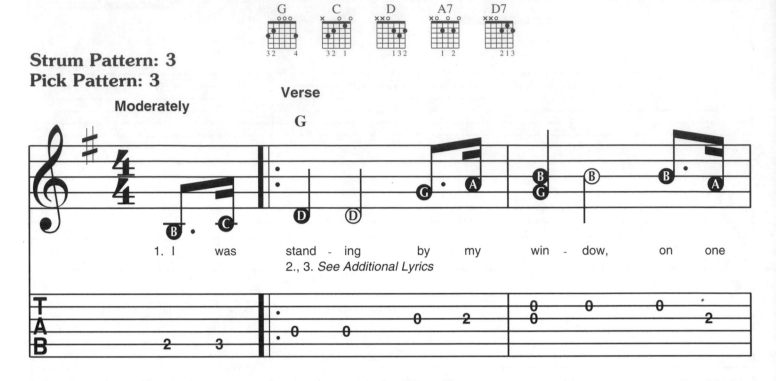

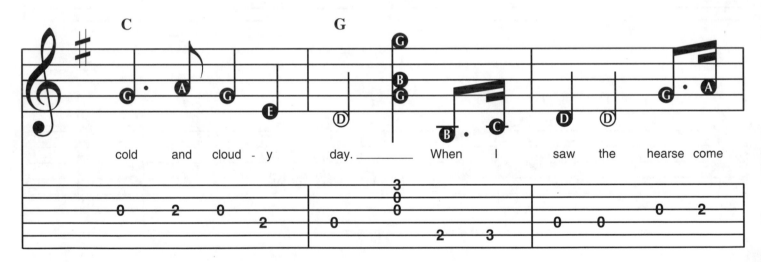

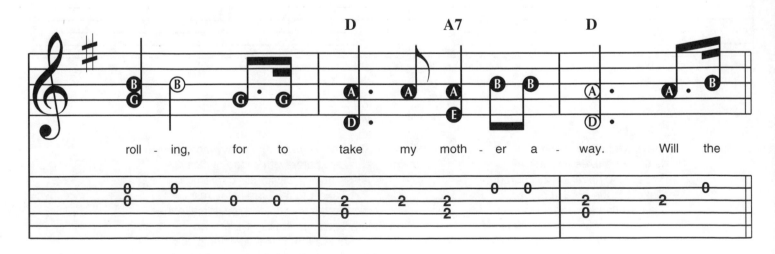

Chorus

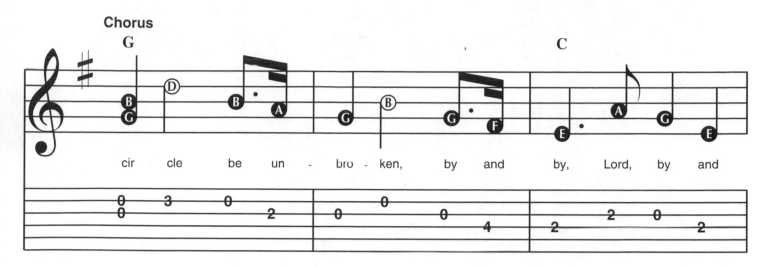

cir - cle be un - bro - ken, by and by, Lord, by and

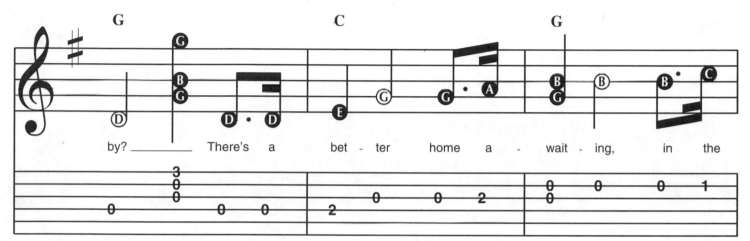

by? _____ There's a bet - ter home a - wait - ing, in the

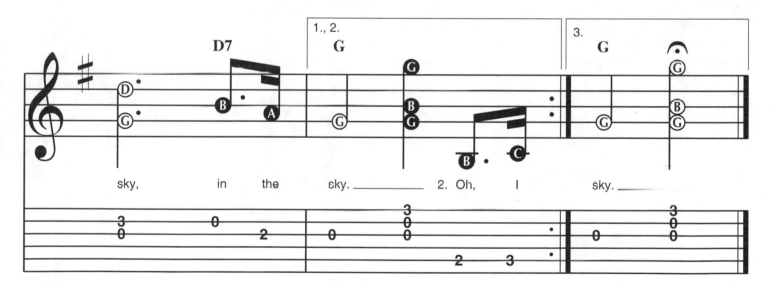

sky, in the sky. _____ 2. Oh, I sky. _____

Additional Lyrics

2. Oh, I told the undertaker,
   "Undertaker please drive slow,
   For this body you are hauling,
   Lord, I hate to see her go."

3. I will follow close behind her,
   Try to hold up and be brave.
   But I could not hide my sorrow,
   When they laid her in her grave.

GREAT CHRISTIAN GUITAR SONGBOOKS

40 SONGS FOR A BETTER WORLD

40 songs with a message, including: All You Need Is Love • Bless the Beasts and Children • Colors of the Wind • Everything Is Beautiful • He Ain't Heavy...He's My Brother • I Am Your Child • Love Can Build a Bridge • What a Wonderful World • What the World Needs Now Is Love • You've Got a Friend • and more.

_____00702068 Easy Guitar with Notes & Tab..................$10.95

BEST OF STEVEN CURTIS CHAPMAN

Features a dozen of his best songs, arranged for fingerstyle guitar: Busy Man • For the Sake of the Call • The Great Adventure • Heaven in the Real World • Hiding Place • His Eyes • His Strength Is Perfect • Hold On to Jesus • I Will Be Here • More to This Life • My Turn Now • What Would I Say.

_____00699138 Fingerstyle Guitar......................$10.95

BEST OF STEVEN CURTIS CHAPMAN FOR EASY GUITAR

15 songs including: The Great Adventure • Heaven in the Real World • His Strength Is Perfect • I Will Be There • More to This Life.

_____00702033 Easy Guitar with Notes & Tab.................$12.95

STEVEN CURTIS CHAPMAN FAVORITES

14 songs, including: Don't Let the Fire Die • Got There with You • Lord of the Dance • Runaway • When You Are a Soldier • and more.

_____00702073 Easy Guitar with Notes and Tab.................$9.95

STEVEN CURTIS CHAPMAN GUITAR COLLECTION

12 of his most popular songs transcribed note-for-note for guitar, including: Fort the Sake of the Call • The Great Adventure • Heaven in the Real World • His Eyes • I Will Be Here • Lord of the Dance • More to This Life • Signs of Life • and more.

_____00690293 Guitar Recorded Versions.......................$19.95

CONTEMPORARY CHRISTIAN FAVORITES

20 great easy guitar arrangements of contemporary Christian songs, including: El Shaddai • Friends • He Is Able • I Will Be Here • In the Name of the Lord • In Christ Alone • Love in Any Language • Open My Heart • Say the Name • Thy Word • Via Dolorosa • and more.

_____00702006 E-Z Guitar With Tab $9.95

CONTEMPORARY CHRISTIAN FAVORITES

17 great songs arranged for fingerstyle guitar: Butterfly Kisses • Chain of Grace • El Shaddai • Friend of a Wounded Heart • Friends • He Is Able • His Strength Is Perfect • Love in Any Language • Open My Heart • Say the Name • Thy Word • Via Dolorosa • more.

_____00699137 Fingerstyle Guitar $9.95

DC TALK – JESUS FREAK

Matching folio with note-for-note transcriptions to this contemporary Christian band's cross-over album. Songs include: Between You and Me • Jesus Freak • In the Light • Colored People • and more. Also includes photos.

_____00690184 Guitar Recorded Versions......................$19.95

DC TALK – SUPERNATURAL

Includes transcriptions in notes & tab of the 13 songs from Supernatural: Consume Me • Dive • Fearless • Godsend • Into Jesus • It's Killing Me • My Friend (So Long) • Red Letters • Since I Met You • Supernatural • There Is a Treason at Sea • The Truth • Wanna Be Loved.

_____00690333 Guitar Recorded Versions......................$19.95

DELIRIOUS? – MEZZAMORPHIS

14 songs in notes & tab from the third album by this Christian punk/pop band from England: Beautiful Sun • Blindfold • Bliss • Deeper 99 • Follow • Gravity • Heaven • It's OK • Jesus' Blood • Kiss Your Feet • Love Falls Down • Metamorphis • The Mezzanine Floor • See the Star. Includes photos.

_____00690378 Guitar Recorded Versions......................$19.95

FAVORITE HYMNS FOR EASY GUITAR

48 hymns, including: All Hail the Power of Jesus' Name • Amazing Grace • Be Thou My Vision • Blessed Assurance • Fairest Lord Jesus • I Love to Tell the Story • In the Garden • Let Us Break Bread Together • Rock of Ages • Were You There? • When I Survey the Wondrous Cross • and more.

_____00702041 E-Z Guitar with Notes & Tab $9.95

GLORIOUS HYMNS

Large, easy-to-read notation and tablature for 30 inspirational hymns: Abide with Me • Amazing Grace • Blessed Assurance • Come Christians Join to Sing • In the Garden • Jacob's Ladder • Rock of Ages • What a Friend We Have in Jesus • more.

_____00699192 EZ Play Guitar $7.95

ALL BOOKS INCLUDE NOTES & TABLATURE

FAVORITES FOR GUITAR

An amazing collection of 50 favorites, including: Amazing Grace • Did You Stop to Pray This Morning • He Lives • His Name Is Wonderful • How Great Thou Art • The King Is Coming • My God Is Real • Nearer, My God, To Thee • The Old Rugged Cross • Take My Hand, Precious Lord • Turn Your Radio On • Will the Circle Be Unbroken • and more.

_____00699374 EZ Guitar with Notes & Tab.....................$14.95

GOSPEL GUITAR

Centerstream Publications

13 popular sacred songs in tab and standard notation, arranged for beginning and intermediate fingerpickers. Songs include: Amazing Grace • Can the Circle Be Unbroken • Just a Closer Walk With Thee • Swing Low, Sweet Chariot • more.

_____00000030 Guitar $7.95

BEST OF AMY GRANT

118 of her best arranged for easy guitar, including: Angels • Baby Baby • Big Yellow Taxi • Doubly Good to You • El Shaddai • Every Heartbeat • Find a Way • Good for Me • House of Love • Lead Me On • Lucky One • Tennessee Christmas • and more.

_____00702099 Easy Guitar with Notes & Tab....................$9.95

GREATEST HYMNS FOR GUITAR

48 hymns, including: Abide with Me • Amazing Grace • Be Still My Soul • Glory to His Name • In the Garden • and more.

_____00702116 Easy Guitar with Notes & Tab....................$7.95

MAKING SOME NOISE
–TODAY'S MODERN CHRISTIAN ROCK

13 transcriptions, including: Big House • Cup • Flood • God • Jesus Freak • Shine • Soulbait • and more.

_____00690216 Guitar Recorded Versions.......................$14.95

THE BEST OF NEWSBOYS

13 songs in notes & TAB from these popular Christian rockers: Breakfast • Breathe • Dear Shame • Entertaining Angels • God Is Not a Secret • I Cannot Get You Out of My System • Real Good Thing • Shine • Spirit Thing • Step up to the Microphone • Strong Love • Take Me to Your Leader • Woo Hoo.

_____00690345 Guitar Recorded Versions.......................$17.95

PRAISE AND WORSHIP FOR GUITAR

25 easy arrangements, including: As the Deer • Glorify Thy Name • He Is Exalted • Holy Ground • How Excellent Is Thy Name • Majesty • Thou Art Worthy • You Are My Hiding Place • more.

_____00702125 Easy Guitar with Notes & Tab $8.95

SONICFLOOD

6 songs transcribed note-for-note, including: Carried Away • Holy One • I Could Sing of Your Love Forever • I Need You • My Refuge • There's Something About That Name.

_____00690385 Guitar Recorded Versions........................$19.95

TODAY'S CHRISTIAN FAVORITES

19 songs, including: Daystar • Find Us Faithful • Go West Young Man • God and God Alone • He Is Exalted • I Will Choose Christ • Jubilate • My Turn Now • A Perfect Heart • Revive Us, O Lord • and more.

_____00702042 Easy Guitar with Notes & Tab $8.95

TODAY'S CHRISTIAN ROCK FOR EASY GUITAR

Over 10 powerful contemporary Christian songs. Includes: Between You and Me (dc Talk) • Flood (Jars of Clay) • Kiss Me (Sixpence None the Richer) • Lord of the Dance (Steven Curtis Chapman) • On My Knees (Jaci Velasquez) • and more.

_____00702124 Easy Guitar with Notes & Tab $8.95